PAUL

PAUL

by
MARTIN DIBELIUS
formerly Professor in the University of Heidelberg

Edited and completed by
WERNER GEORG KÜMMEL
Professor of New Testament, Marburg University

Translated by
FRANK CLARKE

Philadelphia
THE WESTMINSTER PRESS

All rights reserved—no part of this book may be reproduced without permission in writing from the publisher, except by a reviewer who wishes to quote brief passages in connection with a review in magazine or newspaper.

First published 1953
Published simultaneously in Great Britain
by Longmans, Green & Co. Ltd.
New Impressions by Photolithography 1957, 1960,
1962, 1964 and 1966

Tenth printing, 1975

Printed in the United States of America

CONTENTS

	Note by Dr. Kümmel	vii
I.	Paul in History	1
II.	The Jewish and Greek Worlds	15
III.	Paul the Man	27
IV.	Paul Turns to Christ	46
V.	The Mission	67
VI.	The Message and the Churches	85
VII.	Paul's Witness and Theology	102
VIII.	Struggles	125
IX.	The End	141
X.	The Work	154
	General Index	161
	Index of Bible References	169

The Bible text in this publication is from the Revised Standard Version of the Bible, copyrighted 1952 by the Division of Christian Education, National Council of the Churches of Christ in the United States of America, and used by permission.

EDITOR'S NOTE

WHEN Martin Dibelius died on the 11th November 1947, he left six and a half chapters of the manuscript of a small book on Paul which was to be published in the Göschen Collection. Those chapters were almost ready for the press, but of the rest of the manuscript there was nothing except the headings of the chapters and a rough indication of the scope of what was still to be written. As the work that he left was unsuitable for publication in its unfinished state, I willingly accepted Frau Dora Dibelius' suggestion that I should try to take my late teacher's place by revising his manuscript for the press and adding the parts that were still lacking. That manuscript, which went as far as the middle of chapter 7 (page 114), needed little more than verbal revision and, in places, a decision on what the author had intended as his final version. In accordance with his obvious intention, certain parts of chapter 2 were somewhat enlarged; apart from that, nothing was needed except occasionally to correct a slip or fill in a small gap. So, apart from those trifling changes and additions, the text of the first seven chapters (as far as page 114) is as Dr. Dibelius had intended it, and represents his outlook and scholarship. The rest (from page 114) has been added by me. May the last work of a great theologian, which was to form the counterpart of his *Life of Jesus* already published in the Göschen Collection help many to see more clearly the historical figure of the apostle Paul, and to realise his importance in the spiritual struggle of our own time.

WERNER GEORG KÜMMEL.

Zürich, 27th December 1949

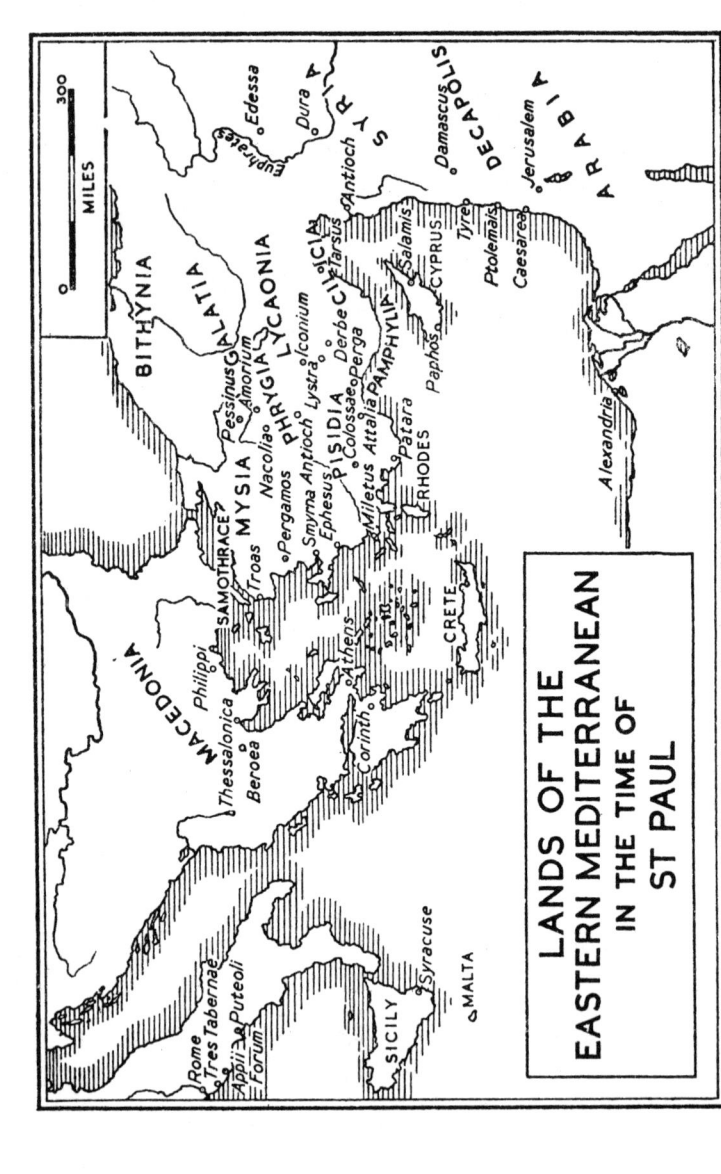

1

PAUL IN HISTORY

OF the apostle Paul, everyone knows that he was the greatest missionary of the Christian faith in the old, classical time of Christianity, that his letters form a considerable part of the New Testament, and that he is therefore still of vital importance to the Church, and indeed to all readers of the Bible, from the most learned to the least. But if we look more closely, we get a divided impression. Paul's work broke open the Jewish framework in which primitive Christianity before him had been confined, and opened the way to winning the non-Jewish world. But it also seems to many that the effect of his letters has been to perpetuate Jewish ideas and assumptions in the Christian Church. Christendom counts Paul among the apostles; but even the original church in Jerusalem never trusted him unreservedly; and after his death the Church, though it certainly read his letters and accepted his ideas, levelled his thoughts down and made them innocuous by incorporating them into its own systems. Since then, in the course of centuries, his real thoughts have again and again been dug up, carried further, and recast. This was done first by Marcion, the great arch-heretic of the second century, who, under Paul's influence, regarded the Law and the gospel as mutually exclusive principles, and attributed them to two different gods, because he misunderstood some of Paul's main ideas. Later, Augustine revived in accordance with his own views the apostle's ideas about sin and grace, and thereby profoundly influenced the character of western Christianity. Finally, not only was Martin Luther's attitude to the doctrine of salvation decisively affected by a passage in the letter to the Romans (1 ^{17}), but his comprehension of Christ was, in its essence, acquired from Paul's letters. Besides these great reactions to Paul, which were most momentous for the history of Christianity, other important effects of his thought should not be forgotten; the founder of the Methodist Church, John Wesley, reached his momentous conversion through Luther's preface to the letter to the Romans; and the pattern of the new theology of the twentieth century, the so-called dialectical theology, was begun by a book on Paul, Karl Barth's "Letters to the Romans".

Nor, in the last hundred years, has there been any lack of those who characterised certain of Paul's essential ideas as a falsification of Christianity or a degeneration of religion, and who thus created a widespread feeling directed against Paul or even against the Christian faith in general. Paul de Lagarde, the great Göttingen scholar, gave significant expression to this feeling in his "German Writings" (1886). He accused Paul, the "completely uncalled" apostle, of a threefold mischievous influence on Christianity: by burdening it with the Old Testament, by introducing into the Church the Pharisaic method of exegesis, and by "bringing into it the Jewish theory of sacrifice and all its connections". These are not meaningless reproaches, and it will be shown later that behind each of the accusations there are certain important questions. After this opposition to Paul from the point of view of the history of religion, there came the psychological opposition of Friedrich Nietzsche. As early as 1880, in his "Red Dawn", he had attributed to Paul, "whose mind was as superstitious as it was cunning", the responsibility for the fact that "the ship of Christianity threw overboard a large part of the Jewish ballast, so that it could and did sail among the Gentiles". Eight years later, in his "Antichrist", he regards the apostle as the "opposite type to the evangelist, the genius in hatred", the "disevangelist", who, with the instinct of the Jewish priest, falsifies history, "arranges for himself, out of a hallucination, the proof that the Redeemer is still alive", and thereby shifts the main interest from this life to the "beyond"—the priest, greedy for power, who domineers over the masses and instructs the flocks.

Much more serious efforts were made by Houston Stewart Chamberlain, in his "Foundations of the Nineteenth Century" (1899), to deal with the problem of Paul; it seemed to him so complicated, that he simply assumed that the apostle's nature consisted of two distinct halves (for that reason he would prefer to regard him as the product of a mixed marriage): a man of Jewish upbringing, full of Jewish conceptions, and bound to the Old Testament way of thought—and yet at the same time so un-Jewish in his doctrine of universal sinfulness and of redemption through "the divine grace that gives faith" (Chamberlain called it "Indo-European") "that he deserves the epithet anti-Jewish". Round that central point, he thought Paul erected a Jewish building, "a kind of latticework", which might be no obstacle when viewed sympathetically, but which became of primary importance for Christianity as the latter developed.

Then, on the basis of a racial theory, Alfred Rosenberg, in his "Myth of the Nineteenth Century", developed Nietzsche's views. For him the "un-Jewish" Paul did not exist. The apostle's ideas meant to him a "bastardising orientalising, and Judaising of Christianity". "Paul quite consciously gathered everything that was politically and morally leprous in his own and other countries, so as to remove all restraint on the exaltation of inferiority." We can almost imagine that we hear Nietzsche speaking; but Nietzsche knew little of recent research about Paul, which was then only at the end of its first stage; in the period between Nietzsche and Rosenberg, however, it has progressed considerably, and, partly by making use of newly discovered evidence about life in ancient times, it has shed fresh light on the essentials of the problems. After that, an arbitrary settlement of them, merely by denunciation, should no longer be possible.

The first scholar of recent times to recognise that Paul's ideas were not to be incorporated into the general Christian theology by being confined to the straightjacket of the Church's traditional interpretation of them and so made innocuous, was Ferdinand Christian Baur of Tübingen, in his book "Paul, the Apostle of Jesus Christ" (1845). Baur and his disciples, in line with the ideas of Hegel, tried to regard the whole of early Christianity as developing out of the contrast between Jewish Christianity and Paulinism. The arguments over this "Tübingen" sketch of early Christianity had a decisive influence on the research of the following decades, and led to a widening of the scope of the problem to include a series of further questions, on which work has been continued till quite recently. From the problem as it was put forward by Baur, there arose a discussion whether the

Paul in History

apostle was more widely and more essentially influenced by Judaism or Hellenism—or by cross-currents of those spheres. Hellenistic Judaism or orientalised Hellenism; what part of his thought is due to the message of Jesus, and what, in fact, was his connection with the historical Jesus of Nazareth? With these historical problems there is also bound up the really fundamental one: whether the core of Paul's doctrine of salvation was the sinner's justification through grace, or the freeing of the world from the invisible powers that oppress it—whether for him salvation consists essentially in present possession, or in the hope of a coming transformation of the world. As all these problems will be discussed in the following chapters, this indication may be enough for the moment. Nor must it be forgotten in this connection, that research on Paul has repeatedly received fresh impetus from other branches of knowledge. The newly awakened appreciation of the later Greek language and literature, the research in Jewish rabbinism, the publication of recently discovered texts, the study of papyri, the history of religion (particularly of Hellenism,), and also modern psychology—all these have contributed to an understanding of Paul, and enriched our picture of him as far as the sources allow.

We know a good deal, comparatively, of Paul's life and thought. Under his name thirteen letters in the New Testament have been handed down to us, and it is with his journeys that the whole of the second half of the Acts of the Apostles is concerned—the same book that has told, in chapter 9, of the conversion of Paul the persecutor of the Christians. But these historical sources have to be examined scientifically like all others, both ancient and modern, before they can be used for the presentation of history.

Paul

The reader of today is apt to be surprised and disconcerted, when he is assured that not all the letters that profess to be Paul's writings are really genuine—that is, composed by the apostle. He first has to get used to the idea that in those days—and not only among Christians—honourable people wrote letters in quite good faith under the name of some well known man, and put them into circulation, either because they imitated his style, or because they used the particular circumstances of his life as an occasion for writing, or because they just appropriated his name for the authorship. Paul too has had spurious letters of that kind ascribed to him. Centuries after his death, a correspondence between him and the philosopher Seneca was invented; on the basis of Col. 4^{16}, a letter from the apostle to Laodicea was constructed, as was a correspondence with the Corinthians, and both were accepted as biblical manuscripts; in the Greek and Syrian Church of the third century, the letter to the Hebrews was incorporated into the New Testament because it was declared to be one of Paul's letters. So we can approach those New Testament writings described as Paul's letters with the question whether all thirteen really do come from him. In fact, at least the two letters to Timothy and the one to Titus (that is, the so-called Pastoral Letters) cannot be used as sources for Paul's life and teaching. They presuppose another Church, which had grown older and more solidly organised than that of his time, with other offices, other opponents, and above all with another Christian ideal of life; to them the tensions that he knew—between this world and the world to come, between the flesh and the Spirit—had already become unfamiliar; for them the Christian life was built up on the "reasonable doctrine" that aims at "good works" and is confirmed by the witness of a good conscience. That is the language of a Christianity of the second or third generation; and if in the second century the heretic Marcion did not receive the Pastoral Letters into his collection of Paul's letters, that perhaps goes to show that their recognition in the Church had not then been fully achieved. Whether genuine fragments of Paul's writings have been worked into these letters cannot be investigated here, and, in fact, can hardly be conclusively proved. It must suffice for us that it has been established that, in trying to understand Paul, we have to disregard the Pastoral Letters. (For a fuller discussion, see my "History of Early Christian Literature", volume II, Göschen Collection, No. 935, pp. 76 ff.).

Of the ten remaining letters of Paul, research has shown that the authenticity of two in particular is not beyond doubt. In the letter to the Ephesians doubts are raised, not so much by its contents as by its relation to the letter to the Colossians, shown both in the similarities and in the differences ("History of Early Christian Literature," II, pp. 30 ff. and 42 ff.). Nor does the letter to the Ephesians, in contrast to Paul's other letters, disclose in detail the circumstances of the correspondence; it is not a letter, but a written communication in the nature of a sermon. Even the name "Ephesus" at the beginning is not mentioned in the oldest manuscripts; and further, the supposition that it was destined for the church at Ephesus (which Paul knew well) is disproved by the text of the letter, which was obviously addressed to a church unfamiliar to the writer. Certain peculiarities in the expression and content of thought, which the letters to the Ephesians and Colossians have in common, seem to be justified in the letter to the Colossians, because that letter helped to combat a newfangled gnostic doctrine; in the letter to the Ephesians there is nothing to account for them. Some researchers solve the problem by denying the authenticity of both letters; others ascribe both to Paul, and regard the impersonal letter to the Ephesians as a circular letter addressed to various communities. It seems to me that the simplest explanation is to regard the letter to the Colossians as one of Paul's writings and to explain its peculiarities by the apostle's peculiar situation, but to regard the letter to the Ephesians as an imitation of the one to the Colossians, and so eliminate it from the various sources of information about Paul's thought.

A peculiar relationship is also cited in the case of the second letter to the Thessalonians, as evidence against its authenticity. But here it is not a question, as in the letters to the Colossians and Ephesians, of striking peculiarities to be found only in these two letters. Here the corresponding passages refer to unimportant things, and the only question that remains open is really whether the apostle wrote the second letter, which was cooler but assumed a closer acquaintance, to the same readers as those for whom the cordial first letter was intended, but who, after this very letter, have to be pictured as new Christians greatly in need of instruction ("History of Early Christian Literature", II, pp. 16 ff.). But before we answer the question by assuming that the letter is not authentic, we should, of course, be careful to see that we do not overlook any of the circumstances in which the correspondence originated. Neither of the two letters to the Thessalonians presents difficulties, if we take them both as coming from Paul. These two letters, then, besides those to the Philippians and Colossians and, in the same group, the short letter to Philemon (in Colossae), and especially the four great letters to Rome, Corinth (two), and the churches in Galatia, are to be regarded as sources for Paul's life and doctrine.

They are sources of the first importance. That is not merely because they were written (or, as we must assume from Rom. 16^{22}, 1 Cor. 16^{21}, and other passages, dictated) by Paul. They are unique because they allow us a glimpse inside his Christian communities, and because at the same time, with their intimate witness, they reveal Paul the man in his faith, thought, and feelings.

Of course, the information about Paul as it is presented in the Acts of the Apostles is not so reliable, since it is not autobiographical; and if it contradicts plain statements in the letters, it has to take second place; the most we can say is that, in certain details, the apostle may have been mistaken. In spite of that, the importance of the accounts in Acts is great. That is particularly true of the information contained in Acts 13–21 about the places that Paul visited on his missionary journeys. Not that there is anything special to relate about all of those places by any means; at the same time, even places that were merely "passed through", such as Amphipolis and Apollonia (Acts 17^1) are also mentioned. Obviously, the author could use notes that a companion had made about the route taken, and perhaps also about the results of the mission, for use in case the journey were undertaken again. The "we" that appears in the account (16^{10-17}; 20^5-21^{18}; and later 27^1-28^{16}) may well indicate that, over some parts of the route, it was the author of Acts himself who drew up these notes. Some have also seen in this "we" an indication of a special source; but there is no difference to be detected, either in style or in matter, between the accounts with "we" and those without it. Indeed, the whole of Acts can be attributed to Luke, one of Paul's companions. It seems to me that this tradition should not be lightly valued; for the book appeared in literary garb—it was dedicated, like the Gospel by Luke, to a certain Theophilus; and really, if the name of the recipient is known, is it right that the name of the giver should be lost?

We therefore have to take it that the author of Acts was in close touch with Paul personally. Of course, that does not mean that everything he tells about him is true down to the smallest detail, still less that Luke understood the apostle's character and theology in all their characteristic features, and expressed that understanding in his narrative. Indeed, as his sketch clearly shows, he was not trying to write a biography of the apostle, but to describe the development and growth of the early Church from its origin in Jerusalem to its expansion as far as Rome. But to him Paul was the great missionary, the archetype who had taken the fateful way of Christianity; and the limitation and emphasis of his material must be understood from that point of view. Besides, when Luke wrote, Paul had already been dead twenty or thirty years (for hints about his death, see Acts 20 $^{22-25, 38}$; 21 ^{11}). Stories about the apostle's activities were obviously widespread among the Christian communities, and Luke sought and collected them, beginning with the story of his conversion. Their historical trustworthiness is, of course, as in all such popular narratives, impossible to determine, but in any case, it varies from one to another; the less we find in them a ready theme for popular narrative, the more we may regard the particular text as reliable. So while the statements about the actual

Paul in History

travelling can be taken as quite reliable, it is only to a limited extent that we can accept the stories as being of real historical value.

Paul's speeches in the Acts have very little biographical value; their importance lies in another direction, as is also the case with speeches in the works of historians (Xenophon, Thucydides, and Josephus). The object of them all is to induce the reader to make certain reflections (though of a very different kind) in certain places. In our case, for instance, the two evangelising sermons in Acts 13 and 17, in the synagogue at Antioch and before the Areopagus, aim at presenting, first and foremost, two types of the early Christian evangelistic speech—typical, of course, rather for the last quarter of the first century, in which Luke wrote, than for the period A.D. 50–60, in which Paul preached. The speeches in which the apostle defends himself, however, in Acts 22, 24, and 26, are intended primarily to serve as apologetics. That can be assumed from the custom of the historians of the time, and inferred from the contents of the speeches. How far Luke possessed any written information about speeches that the apostle had actually made, and whether he worked into them any personal impressions, is difficult to say. Indeed, he had no intention of presenting to his readers the style of Paul's speeches, although he had the experience as well as the gift of style. If we compare the speeches of Peter in Acts 2, 3, and 10 with that of Paul in chapter 13, we see that the author wanted, not to work out the differences between the speakers, but to emphasise the similarity of type. He was more concerned to show how one should preach than to report how Peter or Paul had preached.

So, however little the Acts of the Apostles provides,

or claims to provide, of what we expect today of a historical presentation, and however much its picture of Paul needs to be supplemented and corrected from the apostle's letters, we have no reason to distrust the sketch that it gives of his missionary activities. The author possessed the notes of the journey, and, for certain parts of it, probably his own recollections too. His bias, if one may use the word, was simply to make Paul's missionary route from Antioch to Rome the way appointed by God for Christianity to take from Syria into the middle of the pagan world. It was obviously this view that led him, on the occasion of the important crossing from Asia Minor to Macedonia and Greece (16 $^{6-10}$), to say nothing about the detailed circumstances of the journey, and to explain it solely by the leading of the Spirit. He also treats the apostle's last journey through Greece quite summarily, obviously because it did not take the gospel further into the world (20 $^{1-6}$). On the other hand, he elaborates Paul's journey as a prisoner to Rome (27 ^{1}–28^{16}) at some length and not without regard to literary models, because it signified the triumphal march of Christ to the capital of the world (although, as he himself states, there had already been Christians in Rome for some time). But we have no reason to suppose that Luke's accounts of the two journeys to Asia Minor (13, 14, and 15 ^{36}–16 ^{10}) may be two accounts of the same journey—the author's material preserved him from any such mistakes.

There is, however, a lack of something important for our consideration of Paul's biography; we learn nothing from Acts about either his youth or his end; and this gap in our knowledge is not satisfactorily filled by any information from non-biblical sources. The oldest and most important of such accounts outside the Bible is in

Paul in History

the letter from the church at Rome in the last years of the first century, the so-called "First Epistle of Clement"; according to this, Paul was seven times in chains, he had to flee, he was stoned; on his travels, he reached "as far as the confines of the west", gave his witness before the rulers, and was then "released from the world and received into the holy place, the mightiest example of steadfastness". How much actual knowledge there is behind these words, we shall try to ascertain later (see pp. 150–153).

What is related about Paul in apocryphal literature—parts of it can be read in Hennecke's "Neutestamentliche Apokryphen", second edition—must be regarded as romantic fiction. About one piece of writing which circulated under the title "Acts of Paul" (*Acta Pauli*)—we have known rather more since an incomplete Greek text of these "Acts" was published in 1936 in the Hamburg State and University Library. We find there the story about the lion that was to attack Paul in the arena at Ephesus, but which, endowed with human speech, acknowledged that it was an old friend of the apostle—the one, in fact, that he had once baptised. In these "Acts of Paul" there is also the legend, well known before this recent find, of Saint Thecla, who was won over by Paul to Christianity, but was condemned by the governor of Iconium to be burnt at the stake. But neither fire nor lions and bears nor seals could harm her. The invention of this legend presupposes the widespread veneration of Thecla, already widespread in the eastern Church. That Paul, in these "Acts" preached complete continence as an essential obligation is, in spite of 1 Cor. 7, a gross misrepresentation; that (according to the same source) he never returned to the same mission station is, on the evidence of the epistles (e.g. 2 Cor. 13 [1]) simply erroneous; and that he made the journey to Rome from Corinth as a free man, and not as a prisoner, is, in view of the account in Acts 27, not credible. We know, moreover, through Tertullian (second century), that the author of the "Acts of Paul" was an unknown presbyter in Asia Minor, who himself admitted and acknowledged the invention, saying that what he had done was "only from love of Paul". Thus, for all essential details of Paul's work, we remain dependent on the evidence of the New Testament.

2

THE JEWISH AND GREEK WORLDS

By birth and education, Paul belonged to three different worlds: his Roman citizenship gave him a position of some standing in the great Roman empire, to which the civilisation of Hellenism gave unity; and his native town of Tarsus, besides his missionary work in Asia Minor, Macedonia, and Greece, linked him with that civilisation from his youth onwards. But as he grew up in a community of Hellenistic Jews, he was, in a way, lifted out of that world; for the Judaism of the dispersion (diaspora), in spite of its assimilation to the Hellenistic civilisation, had its own peculiar character, now scoffed at and now respected by other Jews, shunned by some and aspired to by others, notorious for its strange customs, famous for its faith in God and the purity of its morals. Finally, through his further training in Jerusalem, Paul was also brought into contact with the body of scribes in Palestine. Thus he was at the same time a Roman citizen, a Hellenistic Jew, and a Jerusalem scribe; and we now have to consider the significance of this.

Tarsus, the town where Paul was born (Acts 9 [11], 21 [39], 22 [3]) was the centre of the considerable traffic of the Cilician plain, connected by passes over both the Taurus and the Amanus Mountains with the Hellenistic world of Asia Minor as well as with the Semitic country of Syria, neither a large town nor really a commercial town, but, by virtue of its position as a centre of communications, of some account and also culturally important. Jerome (about 400) mentions a piece of hearsay, according to which Paul's parents had lived at Gischala in Galilee, the capture of which had caused them to be transported to Tarsus. In that case, Paul's avowal that he was "a Hebrew born of Hebrews" (Phil. 3 [5]) would mean that the family had only recently become Jews of the dispersion, that Paul's father had probably been a prisoner of war, and that perhaps when he was released he had (as often happened) obtained the Roman citizenship that Paul, according to Acts 22 [28], had already inherited.

The civilisation of Hellenism, which was still of decisive importance for the first centuries of the empire, was determined by universalism and syncretism, being directed towards uniformity and also towards a blending with what was foreign, especially with what was oriental. The unity of language was created, as Greek, divesting itself of the peculiarities of dialect, developed into a universal language (Greek *koine*) common to all. The unity of the Mediterranean world was expressed in a system of good traffic routes that made travelling easy even for the unimportant man who went on foot with his cloak (Acts 20 [13]; 2 Tim. 4 [13]). To that, moreover, the Roman empire added a centralisation of power, besides a legal code that assumed precedence over local laws; there was now uniformity, too, in money, weights, and measures; and besides that, inside the empire's frontiers, which were pushed further and further out, there was a continual increase of traffic in consequence

The Jewish and Greek Worlds

of the frequent movement of troops and transfer of officials. The importance of all that for spreading the Christian faith is obvious; and there is really no need to ask how the Roman church could have originated. Tradespeople, slaves in an official's retinue may have taken Christianity to Rome even in the thirties and forties; and it is no wonder that, as we learn from the letter to the Romans, there were Christians in Rome before Paul (and Peter) went there. Particularly early evidence of the intermixing of religions, the so-called syncretism, comes from the time of the threat from Hannibal, which caused the black stone of Rhea, mother of the gods (in Asia Minor) to be removed from Pessinus to Rome, where her temple was dedicated on the Palatine Hill in 191 B.C. A hundred years later the influence of foreign deities, particularly the Egyptian Isis and the Persian Mithras, began to grow in the Roman army, which then, in the first centuries of the Christian era, set up its shrines to the bull-slaying Persian god in the whole of the Roman empire as far as the Danube countries and south-west Germany. In Greece, the oriental influence had met the later Greek development, which had in some respects taken the same direction. By the idea of cosmopolitanism and the doctrine of the *logos*—the supreme wisdom governing the universe—the Stoic philosophy, whose great teachers nearly all came from the east, had prepared the ground on which the naturalisation and philosophic interpretation of foreign deities—Isis, Osiris, the Egyptian Hermes Trismegistus (i.e., the Egyptian god Thoth), and Attis—could be carried through. The resuscitation of certain oracles, the preference given to the more mysterious of the Greek gods, such as Dionysus, the spread of the Orphic sect with its dedications and its belief in another

Paul

world, created a religious romanticism open to all foreign cults, even those with customs of barbaric origin and aspect (such as the circumcision of the Jews, and the castration of the priests of Attis and the Syrian goddess), because crude and savage rites were supposed to have a mysterious meaning behind them.

All these foreign religions came into the west as private cults, and were characterised by the name that was also given to the exclusive Greek cults of Demeter, Dionysus, and Orpheus: mysteries. One was not born into them; one applied for admission, and, if the deity approved, was initiated, to go through life then as an initiate (*mystes*) partaker of the mystery, belonging entirely to that particular deity. One now shared in the divine life, was assured of divine protection, and was freed from the pressure of the power of fate. The Hellenic race had felt itself threatened by the latter in increasing measure, since, in consequence of the widening of all relationships, it had lost the old ties of the city state, the cult of the state, and a regulated social status. The individual felt himself tossed about by the blind power of fate, till the deity to whom he surrendered himself as a devotee granted him the grace of a new existence. The initiation into a mystery therefore brought to people, without distinction of rank, a new nobility and deliverance, through divine grace, from the powers of fate. The strange cults would not have exercised this power of attraction if there had not been a widespread need of such deliverance; and here again the two worlds met, the west and the east. The Greek world, which had grown old, also knew the need, but not to the full extent till after its own native cells, with their own particular cults, had lost their separate existence;

The Jewish and Greek Worlds

the religions of the east, on the other hand, were more or less built up on it, as the Oriental had a different relation to the deity. For in that relation the Oriental was conscious of complete dependence; he knew that his obligation was that of a slave, and so he called the deity his "lord" (Greek *kyrios*), while the Greek and Roman, with all their fear of the divine, never regarded the gods as absolute lords, or man as completely dependent and subservient.

It is true that the communities in which these oriental deities were worshipped were not always clearly marked off from each other by a rigid division into cults. Many of the mystery deities had been combined, especially among educated people, with the theory of revealed knowledge (Greek *gnosis*); and consequently the old myths about the gods had been reinterpreted into revelations about the origin of heaven and earth, about the secrets of the soul and of the world of spirits, and about man's destiny after death. The oriental myth about the "first man", who, having come from heaven, had entangled himself in material things, but whom heaven had rescued and restored with his spiritual self to the celestial world, suggested to many who were longing for deliverance an explanation of their own subjection to the material world and a hope of emancipation into the heavenly world, to which they tried to rise through mystical meditation or ecstasy. As these gnostic speculations could combine with the most diverse religions, and even with Jewish revealed religion, Paul was bound, sooner or later, to meet this religious philosophy in his churches, and come to grips with it (see pp. 135–140).

Judaism too had been received as an eastern religion into the Hellenistic world—in fact, fairly early. Since the end of the Babylonian captivity, which had established a considerable dispersion in Babylon, Jews had streamed into the inhabited parts of the Mediterranean countries, especially into the towns. For it was not, in the main, rural colonists who founded the Judaism of the dispersion, but townspeople whose movement was caused chiefly by a flourishing trade, though also by military service and deportation, and perhaps by being made prisoners of war (see p. 16); they penetrated to Egypt, Syria, and Asia Minor, to Greece and Italy, and at last as far as Gaul and Spain. It was not till after the exile, that is about 500 B.C., that there began the twofold development that has characterised world-Jewry: its separation from the land and agriculture, and its close connection with commerce; it was not till then that there began the separation from political history, which, except for the short Maccabean period in the second century B.C., is linked with the renunciation of a Jewish state. Before the exile, Israel and Judah were small states with an agricultural population, and the trading people were the Phoenicians; but afterwards the Jews of the dispersion took over their inheritance. These Jews broke away from their homeland in an even more radical way: they adopted the common language, the *koine*-Greek, in which they wrote their Bible—the so-called Septuagint, because, according to tradition, it was the work of seventy translators; and they also created their own national literature, which came to be widely read by non-Jews too. In fact we have known, since the synagogue of Dura-Europos on the Euphrates was excavated in 1932–33, that here and there they so far adapted their customs to those of the people among whom they lived as to break the Old Testament pro-

The Jewish and Greek Worlds

hibition of images; for about A.D. 230 all the walls of the synagogue there were decorated from top to bottom with pictures representing scenes from the Old Testament, not only freely portraying human figures, but sometimes going so far as to add, as a decoration, those of naked people and pagan gods. To be sure, the ultimate object of those representations, which are in parts very impressive and carried out with a wealth of imagery, was to proclaim God's dealings with his people by which he brings them salvation in history and at the last day.

The result of this was that numerous non-Jews attended the Jewish services; some to become merely attenders (they are called God-fearing in Acts 13 [16, 26])—these had to observe certain ordinances regarding cleanliness, and keep the sabbath; others, by being circumcised and baptised, to become proselytes, that is full and equal members of the Jewish community; these had to keep the whole Jewish law, and took firm root in the Jewish people by marrying from among them. There was therefore no trace of any attempt in the Judaism of the dispersion to maintain racial purity; the orders of Ezra and Nehemiah to the community at Jerusalem as to the dissolution of mixed marriages, were forgotten, and with good reason, because the important thing to these Jews was religion, not race.

It is unlikely that Paul would have become the great Christian missionary if his home had not been in this wider Judaism, if he had not been able to read and write Greek and possessed the Septuagint as his Bible, if he had not been used to accommodating himself to foreign customs, and if he had not had an eye for the wider world of highways by land and sea and for the great cities of the Mediterranean world. But also for Jerusalem—that was a matter

Paul

of course for him, especially if his family originally came from Palestine. Even the mass of the Jews of the dispersion did not entirely lose their connection with Palestine and Jerusalem, for it was maintained from there by means of messengers of the central religious authority, the Sanhedrin. In Jerusalem there was the temple, the only place where the Jew might sacrifice, and therefore the only real place of worship (in the ancient sense) of Judaism. But it was in Jerusalem too, that all those activities were cultivated and developed that made up Jewish piety after the exile: study, instruction, and compliance with the Law. The first of these was the concern of the scribes; the last was that of all pious Jews, especially those who claimed to be pious in a special sense, and who therefore separated themselves from the unlearned and called themselves "separated people"—Pharisees. To this group Paul, and perhaps his father before him, belonged (Acts 23 ^{6}); and of that essential part of his life it may be said that Paul would not have become the radical Christian who freed Christianity from the religion of the Law, if he had not known what bondage to the Law meant, and known it better, more deeply, and more consistently than the disciples of Jesus.

The strict Jew in the Pharisaic sense was bound to feel that his compliance with the Law was an all-embracing obligation: everyone who accepts circumcision "is bound to keep the whole law" (Gal. 5 ^{3}). The really tragic nature of this idea, in view of the question whether it is at all possible to carry out such an obligation, probably never occurred to the average Pharisee. When he had to admit that some legal requirements remained unfulfilled and that some failures unwittingly occurred, he drew strength and comfort from reading in the Old

The Jewish and Greek Worlds

Testament what is written there of the grace of God (see p. 34); and the distressing realisation of insufficiency in face of the Law's innumerable demands—we find it in the apocryphal fourth book of Esdras, where it is particularly impressive, and also among some of the rabbis—is even there repeatedly overborne by the faith that one belonged to the chosen people for whom God's promises held good, and who could therefore lay claim to God's grace. It is true that, as a Christian, Paul wrote as if he had never, during his pre-Christian life, known those ideas about God's grace; but it may be that the convert saw the logical conclusions of the religion of the Law more sharply and single-mindedly than he could have seen them before.

Speaking generally, the picture of the Judaism of Palestine before the destruction of Jerusalem in A.D. 70 is richer than one would infer from the words of Jesus against the Pharisees and from the letters of Paul. In the first place, some of the scribes were less rigid and less consistent representatives of a strict legalism. As long as they could support their opinions by reference to passages in the Bible, they were not classed as heretics; and indeed, with the prevailing technique of exegesis, the sacred book could be made to produce proofs for everything. The heretics were those who broke the commands of the Law by their actions (or led others to do so)—broke the sabbath, for instance, or ate the flesh of an animal that had not been slaughtered in the orthodox way, or frequented the houses of Gentiles without "purifying" themselves afterwards, or broke one of the ten commandments without being protected by some special interpretation of the text; for in purely legalistic religions offences of ritual or ethics are always regarded as worse than deviations from dogmatic doctrines. That is why relations were so strained between the representatives of a strict legalism (the Pharisees) and the mass of the people, who, while assenting in principle to their doctrines, were unable, because of the daily burden of their work, either to acquire the necessary knowledge of the Law or to fulfil the immense number of its requirements involving every aspect of their lives. It was to that majority, the "people of the land" (Hebrew *am haaretz*), as the sticklers for the Law contemptuously called them, that Jesus and his disciples belonged, and it was in those circles of the "poor" that the piety of the psalms and prophets had had its home. Lastly, besides the world of legalism there was the cult of the temple—another means of access to God, perhaps to the mind of ancient times a more venerable and more certain means. For Jewish piety in the time of Jesus reached out in two directions: one was the worship of the one holy God, who had made his name to dwell in a place on earth—"a temple of the one God, common to all, just as God himself is common to all" (that is how the Jewish historian Josephus has it in his work "Against Apion", II, 193); the other was the subordination of one's whole life to the commandment "You shall be holy to me, for I the Lord am holy" (Lev. 20 ^{26}). And while the protagonists of legalism, the Pharisees, were regarded by the people as specially pious, the members of the priestly nobility, called Sadducees, also preserved their authority, both in the Sanhedrin and in their relations with Rome, the occupying power, to which Judaea and Samaria had been subject since the deposition of Herod's son Archelaus in A.D. 6 [1]

---

[1] In Galilee and Peraea, another of Herod's sons, Antipas, ruled under Roman sovereignty; and lastly, one of Herod the Great's grandsons, Agrippa I, united (with the support of the Romans) the whole of Palestine under his

The Jewish and Greek Worlds

On the other hand, we must not overlook in this connection the existence of certain special groups on the fringe of Judaism, the most important being the order of the Essenes, who lived apart, according to their own particular customs, in settlements as well as in towns. The discipline of the order was based on ascetic, moral, ritualistic, and communistic rules. Its non-Jewish elements seem, as far as we know, to have been its own form of sun-worship, and a sacred meal of special food, of which the brothers of the order, dressed in sacred clothing, partook in absolute silence. That suggests a sacrament or a mystical celebration; and although Paul had nothing to do with the Essenes, we may yet ask, in view of his Christian piety, whether the Judaism in which he grew up contained anything comparable to mysticism. Some mystical interpretations of writings, as put forward by the greatest writer of the Judaism of the dispersion, Philo of Alexandria, seem to point to it; but we do not know whether Philo was merely expressing his own views, or whether he had a community behind him. In itself, Pharisaic Judaism was a stranger to mysticism, for it did not feel the need to seek union with the deity in a non-rational sphere, as another and more rational way was open to it: that of action. It is possible, however, that somewhere outside official Judaism a special cult of mystical piety may have been kept up, just as on the fringe of Judaism there existed, for instance, groups that attributed a certain significance to ablutions and other ceremonies, and just as gnostic speculations combined quite early with legalistic piety—a fact with which Paul was confronted on occasions in his churches.

---

rule for a short time (A.D. 41–44; see Dibelius "Jesus", Göschen Collecttion 1130, p. 29). But these political events were of no importance for the main structure of Judaism.

Probably not far removed from such sects was the movement of John the Baptist which forms the starting-point for the history of Christianity.

3

PAUL THE MAN

IN the first decade after the death of Jesus, the position of nascent Christianity was not yet clarified, because its frontiers were still undefined. In Jerusalem there was a community of his followers, who were waiting for their Master's return in glory from heaven, and who, moreover, were more closely united to Judaism than he himself had been. But there were also, in Antioch and other places, Christian believers who had recognised Jesus as the Christ and as the completion of the Jewish religion on a higher plane—people who had formerly been Jews of the dispersion, and were now, like them, all the more willing to receive into their community those of Gentile birth. Into this strangely divided Church there came a decisive influence, clarifying, invigorating, and significant for the future; and the man who brought it was Paul.

Paul had this advantage over all the other apostles of Jesus, that he was a Pharisee trained in the Law, and was therefore in a much better position to realise what a contrast to the Jewish world the gospel of Jesus presented. But over most of the Pharisees he had the further advantage that he came from Greek Judaism, and so knew more of the world, and understood more of its thought and language, than did the guardians of the Law in

Jerusalem. These two advantages were necessary in the first place for his historical achievement; for without the first he would not have become the great prophet of the Christian faith, and without the second he would not have become the successful missionary. If we want to understand that achievement, we must first see what kind of man he really was.

In the apocryphal "Acts of Paul" mentioned above (see pp. 13, 14) there is a description of the apostle: "Short of stature, bald and bow-legged, vigorous, with meeting eyebrows and a prominent nose, and full of friendliness; indeed at one moment he looked like a man, and at the next he seemed to have the appearance of an angel." It can hardly be proved, however, that this is anything more than the description of a Jew in a somewhat glorified portrait, as is right and proper in the case of the apostle, who is the hero of the book.

That brings us to a question that is sometimes asked today, whether Paul was really Jewish by race. He himself, at least, held that he was: "Of the people of Israel . . . a Hebrew born of Hebrews"—that is how he described himself (Phil. 3 [5]). In the same way, he referred to the Jews as his "kinsmen by race" (Rom. 9 [3]), and knew that he himself was one of that people,"a descendant of Abraham, a member of the tribe of Benjamin" (Rom. 11 [1]). The only clue that might possibly justify a different view leads to Gischala in Galilee, from where, according to Jerome's remark already mentioned (see p. 16), Paul's family was said to have emigrated. If that information were correct, one might ask whether in Galilee, with its largely foreign population, it would be safe to assume that the family was of purely Jewish origin. We must therefore allow for the possibility that it was not;

but this possibility does not mean that there need be any serious doubt about the matter.

The question of racial origin is a matter of general interest as regards Paul, but it is less strong than in the case of Jesus. Many people wish to take Jesus away from any connection with Judaism; they think that is the only way in which they can understand the gospel. On the other hand, far from wishing to "rescue" Paul's message, they would rather remove it from our world altogether; they think they must pillory it as typically Jewish, not detach it from its connection with Judaism. In any case, this connection does exist, even if Paul should not have been of purely Jewish race; for the presuppositions of his thought are Jewish and not Greek; but they are diaspora-Jewish (the difference has already been made plain in chapter 2). For, as has already been stressed, Paul was born at Tarsus in Cilicia (see p.15); and, as his father possessed Roman citizenship (see p.16), it can be assumed that his family had a certain standing in Tarsus. Further, even if we allow that it must remain uncertain whether his father was connected with the Pharisees' community in the Jews' native country, we can see from the course of Paul's education that even as a boy, Saul or Paul was heir to a strict and orthodox Judaism. Saul or Paul—that is what we have to call him; for the supposition, which has become widespread, that it was only through his conversion that Saul became Paul, does not agree with Acts (13 ^{9}), which does not begin to call him Paul till just before the beginnning of the notes about the journeys, these notes probably being responsible for the change. But that again occurs too early to justify the old supposition that the apostle called himself Paul after the proconsul Sergius Paulus of Cyprus, whom he won for Christianity; for Sergius Paulus is not converted before Acts 13 [12]. In fact, everything we know about naming among the Jews, as well as what we can infer from the wording of Acts 13 [9], where the name Paul is introduced, leads us to assume that Paul had both names from birth: Saul, the name of the king, from the same tribe (Benjamin) to which the apostle belonged (Rom. 11 [1]), and the Roman name Paul, probably chosen because of its similarity. It was a frequent practice among the Jews at that time, and has been up to the present, to use two names at the same time, one in the synagogue, and another in the world at large—a Joshua would be called Jason; a Silas, Silvanus; and a John, Mark.

Paul was probably born about the beginning of our era. In the letter to Philemon, which was written between 55 and 60, he calls himself an old man (Philem. [9]); but according to the ideas of those days, anyone over 50 could so describe himself. The Acts of the Apostles mentions him for the first time at the stoning of Stephen (7 [58]), and speaks of him as a young man; the event took place between 30 and 35, and the description suggests a "young man" at least 24 years old, and perhaps slightly older. Paul grew up in his native town Tarsus (p. 15), and certain elements in his education show that he had shared in the Hellenistic civilisation of his native land. Here his manipulation of the Greek language should be particularly noted—his writings are not in literary Greek; but this essentially popular style of his letters, though in marked contrast to the more polished diction of his speeches recorded in Acts, shows in forms, constructions, plays on words, antithesis, and images signs of a more elevated speech, such as we find particularly in the popular rhetoric of the Stoic and Cynic itinerant

Paul the Man

preachers, and indeed of Epictetus, who was a generation later than Paul. Where he does not lose himself in laborious demonstrations and complicated expositions, Paul's language is alive, going straight to the heart, and of an originality and force that had long been missing from the literature of his time. The use, too, of the Greek Bible in quotations, allusions, and reminders points to an author who was at home in Greek. In his writings, the influence of philosophic doctrines can be traced only in brief allusions (Rom. 1 [19, 20]; 2 [14]; Phil. 4 [8]), and in the use of certain conceptions such as conscience, nature, and duty. One must take care not to over-emphasise these Greek elements in his education. Paul's writings are lacking in quotations from the higher literature, for the one line taken from Menander's comedy "Thaïs" and not given as a formal quotation (1 Cor. 15 [33]) may have become a proverb. It is a completely different and more polished way in which Acts makes Paul speak and quote, particularly before the Areopagus (Acts 17 [28]). And if the real Paul uses images of athletic contests, as particularly in 1 Cor. 9 [25-27], we must not therefore assume that he often attended such exhibitions; for these, like the images of military life, or of milk and solid food, or of the body (1 Cor. 14 [8]; 3 [2]; 12 [12-27]) were the common property of popular philosophers, whose sermons could be heard in the streets and squares of Tarsus, as in other Hellenistic towns. Perhaps, indeed, the young Jew did not need to stop and listen to them; it is certain that that kind of popular rhetoric had merged into the eloquence that was practised in the Greek-speaking congregations of the synagogues; and so it is quite possible that Saul-Paul received Greek too through the medium of Judaism.

First and foremost, however, the inheritance that he had received was Jewish—the central importance of a belief in the holy and righteous God, and the ordering of one's life and thought according to his law. But this, which was common to all orthodox Judaism in the motherland of Palestine as well as outside in the dispersion, came to Paul in Tarsus at first in a markedly Hellenistic form; indeed, it was in the Greek language that he first received it from the synagogue there. The fact that Jews of today, coming directly from rabbinism, feel that there is something strange and un-Jewish about Paul's letters, is connected with this Hellenistic part of his inheritance. In fact, neither the speculation about the first and last man (1 Cor. 15 $^{45, 46}$) nor the interpretation of the story of Hagar and Sarah (Gal. 4 $^{22-31}$) in terms of the Jewish and Christian relation to God could find a place in the Talmud. On the other hand, we should not think of this kind of Hellenistic Judaism as being that of the typical Hellenistic expositor of the Old Testament, Philo of Alexandria. Even if we leave out of account everything that separates the latter from Paul the Christian, we still find great differences in their valuation of the Law. The Alexandrian traces the legal instructions back to man's general ideas, and at the same time explains the narratives of Genesis by the mystical life of the individual soul with God; here too he is striving to demonstrate the cultural value of the Old Testament in a philosophic sense. The apostle, on the other hand, sees in the Old Testament the rigorous demands of God, and also his revelations of the destiny of the people of Israel and mankind; and so he shows himself much less ready for a Hellenising reinterpretation of the sacred book.

Paul the Man

That is no doubt connected with the fact that it was in the Jewish motherland, in Jerusalem itself, that Paul was schooled in the doctrines of the Law. According to Acts 22 [3], he was "brought up in this city at the feet of Gamaliel, educated according to the strict manner of the law of our fathers". That sounds almost as if he had gone to Jerusalem when he was still a child; but in view of the Hellenistic elements in this thought, such an assumption would probably not be correct. His parents may have remained in Tarsus, but Saul-Paul went as a young man to Jerusalem, to receive a rabbinical higher education. If the family had actually immigrated into Cilicia from Palestine, and if it happened that not only Paul's sister's son (Acts 23 [16]) but the sister herself lived in Jerusalem, such a move is quite intelligible; but even apart from that, one can understand that the capital of Judaism attracted a Pharisee. In looking back on that time, Paul describes himself "as to righteousness under the law blameless" (Phil. 3 [6]), and as having "advanced in Judaism beyond many of my own age among my people, so extremely zealous was I for the traditions of my fathers" (Gal. 1 [14]). From that, one must not assume forthwith that he was a fully trained rabbinical scholar, an ordained judge; an indication to the contrary comes in particular from the fact that, as a Christian, he draws a one-sided picture of Jewish doctrine. That may be due partly to the prophetic power of his message, which aimed only at illuminating the revelation that had been given him, and partly to the psychology of the convert, which made him see his life before the great turning as a wrong road leading to disaster. But those two reasons do not give an adequate explanation. When Paul sets every Jew the task of keeping the whole Law inviolable (Gal. 5 [3]), but at the same time asserts that no mortal is "justified by works of the law" (Gal. 2^{16}; Rom. 3 ^{20}), he has stated in the most striking terms the fundamental demand that characterised the religion of the Law; but an orthodox pupil of the rabbis would have been bound to remember that its doctrine also gave a certain place to forgiving love. God's word to Moses: "I will be gracious to whom I will be gracious" (Ex. 33 ^{19}) would be understood in a rabbinical commentary to mean that God indeed gave to the deserving man according to merit, but bestowed his grace on the undeserving as a free gift (*Tanchuma*, ed. Buber, Ki tissa § 16, p. 116). Paul, however, heard in the same word the proclamation of the absolute will of God, who chooses freely on whom he will have mercy, and whom he "hardens" (Rom. 9 $^{15, 18}$). Nor is this view of individual predestination the orthodox Jewish one; the rabbis regarded as the object of choice the "chosen" people; and membership of it or of its pious nucleus—that is what the Pharisees felt themselves to be—gave to the individual the guarantee of salvation. Examples have already been given (see p. 32) to show that the way in which Paul uses the Old Testament is not always that of the rabbis.

In the range of ideas that would come with special force to the average Pharisee there is also the strong emphasis on the apocalyptic hope. That would be a matter of course with a Christian apostle; but what strikes one in Paul's case is that, regarding the coming of the Messiah, he says things that he could not have learnt either from the Christian community or from the rabbinic teachers; examples can be found in 1 Cor. 15; 2 Thess. 2; 1 Cor. 2; and Col. 1. It is a question here partly of elements of popular belief, but partly, too, of

Paul the Man

speculations such as were fostered in the Judaism of the dispersion and occur again in gnostic writings. The rabbis, on the other hand, have no complete eschatology; they treat individual questions in that sphere in their own way, combining them with chronological computations and exegetical details; and that is no wonder, for in the realm of their interpretation and fulfilment of the Law there is no real eagerness about the future, as interest is monopolised by the present and its duties, large and small. From this point of view too, therefore, it is open to doubt whether the Judaism into which Paul grew, and which he adopted with such passionate zeal, really was the orthodox rabbinical one. The same question would have to be considered with regard to the ideas that are described in Paul the Christian as mystical or gnostic, and which give his Christian piety its characteristic ring—if only we knew whether he had entertained such ideas and sentiments before he became a Christian. It is possible to hold the opinion that it is a question merely of a part of his mental equipment, and one that had not shown itself in his pre-Christian days; one can certainly point to the presence of mystical ideas in Hellenistic Judaism, especially in the writings of Philo, and assume that Paul was influenced by currents of that kind. If so, he would not have been a rabbinical Jew in that respect either; for mysticism does not thrive where no other service of the eternal God is known than the fulfilling of his commandments.

To mention another conclusion of biographical importance, to be drawn from the view that we are considering: a rabbinical teacher would probably have felt obliged, in accordance with the Talmud, to marry early; and so people have occasionally tried to make Paul into a widower, since he indicates in 1 Cor. 7 that he is unmarried. But this very chapter shows clearly the perplexity in which Paul found himself in relation to the question of marriage: he, as an unmarried man and an enthusiast for celibacy, is to recommend marriage to the Corinthians on the grounds of spiritual well-being. We can see his embarrassment from the way in which he distinguishes between command and permission, between the word of the Lord and his own advice, and in which finally, without relying on the apostolic authority that he stresses elsewhere, he supports his opinion with the modest sentence: "and I think that I have the Spirit of God". Anyone who finds such difficulties in this question has no first-hand experience of marriage: Paul was a bachelor, not a widower.

The statement in Acts 22 [3] must therefore be regarded as one-sided as far as it makes Paul an orthodox pupil of the rabbis, and this verse gives us no reason to assume that he had been taken to Jerusalem when he was still a child. The fact is that Saul-Paul was subjected, first, in Tarsus, to the influences of Hellenistic Judaism, and secondly, in Jerusalem, to those of the rabbis. The tradition that he had been a pupil of Gamaliel need not be disputed on that account, only there is no need to make him into an ordained judge, even in connection with the martyrdom of Stephen and the journey to Damascus. It is usual to identify the Gamaliel of Acts with the person generally called Rabban Gamaliel I in the Talmud; but for chronological reasons this is not quite certain. It is certain, however, that Paul was a Pharisee and was schooled in the doctrines of the Law, and that, in spite of all the qualifications that we have had to make here, he owed a large part of his intellectual

Paul the Man

equipment to the Pharisaic circle and to Judaism as a whole.

In Tarsus he had, in fact, grown up in Pharisaic Judaism. That also involved learning a trade. In Acts 18 [3] that trade is described with a word that means "tent-maker", but which the writers of the early Church explain as "leather-worker". Paul, however, must not be regarded as having the social status of a manual worker; the Jew who intended to devote himself to the service of the Law learnt a trade for the sake of his independence. Paul the Jew, moreover, accepted as a matter of course a good many ideas and customs that may have seemed strange to his Gentile Christian churches. He did not find it objectionable that Jews, especially in Palestine, should still live, eat, and pray according to the Jewish usage when they became Christians—only they must not make a merit of it before God, or impose the same customs on their fellow-Christians of non-Jewish origin—among Christians, national customs were not again to become religious works. Perhaps from this point of view we can understand, in their relation to each other, certain actions that are reported among his apostolic activities, although critical research has often asserted their inconsistency. In Gal. 2 [3] Paul stresses the fact that the Gentile Christian Titus, who was his companion on the journey to the apostle's conference, had not been made to undergo circumcision in Jerusalem. But in 16 [3] Acts tells us that when Paul chose the Christian Timothy, who was half Jewish, to help him in his missionary work, he had him circumcised "because of the Jews that were in those places" (referring to the towns of Lystra and Iconium in Asia Minor). The fact was that, as Timothy was of half Jewish birth, it would not do to let the Jews regard him, in that missionary work, as an apostate. The circumcision of Titus in Jerusalem, however, would have involved the admission that the Jewish rite was obligatory, and therefore meritorious, for Christians. We shall therefore be able to understand both these incidents historically from Paul's peculiar position; but in that case there is no ground for dispute, especially as it is difficult to imagine that that brief note about Timothy could have been invented; elsewhere the Acts takes no special notice of him, and mentions him only together with other people.

The account, too, in the same book (21 $^{23-26}$) of how Paul is said to have taken part in some way, as a Christian, in releasing from their vows four Jewish Christians in the temple at Jerusalem, can perhaps pass as authentic, although it has been contested by critics. The Christian apostle wants to show that he pays respect to the Law of his fathers, and that he does not prohibit such people as Jewish Christians in the mission field from following its precepts—always provided that they do not regard such observance as meritorious, or demand it from Gentile Christians. Who can say whether Paul himself did not keep to the Jewish ritual of prayers in his own private life? The radical nature of his faith was shown in another matter, and one must be careful not to put him down as a "Protestant". At least once in his letters he took for granted a Jewish custom even in the churches of Gentile Christians, the reason being that it was in force in all the Christian churches: this was when he forbade the women of Corinth to pull down the veil covering their hair, when they were in prophetic ecstasy or praying extempore (1 Cor. 11 $^{2-16}$). If we understand the text aright, he based the custom of the veil on the explanation that had been given to him as a Jewish boy: if the woman, the weaker sex, presses forward into the heavenly sphere, she has to ward off the angels that press in on her or obstruct her. This she does with the veil, which possesses magic power over spirits, and is therefore the "power" on her head. We can bring these ideas to life only from existing parallels in the history of religion; for Paul, however, they were alive, because an ancient religion was part of one's life in the world in which he had grown up.

All those things, however, are trifles compared with the main thing that he learnt from Judaism, and which he learnt so thoroughly that he recognised, as no one before him had recognised, its incompatibility with the Christian faith: namely, the basing of salvation on the Law, and the consequent concentration of the whole of life on the Law. He would never have preached Christ so whole-heartedly and unreservedly if he had not previously been such an earnest Jew, and even as a Christian, he kept one thing inviolable: the conviction of the divine origin of the Law. Even to the Christian Paul, the whole of the Old Testament remained the book of revelation, from which the only true knowledge of God was received —even if, in consequence of infection by sin, its precepts had brought to men condemnation instead of salvation; and he therefore felt it an urgent matter to understand the book, and to understand it better, if possible, than the Jews understood it. But when he plunged into details, it was natural for him to use against the Jews the exegetical technique that he had learnt among them. Thus we find in his letters some of the rules used that we know from the rabbinic literature as expository rules: the inference from the difficult to the easy, the combining of all kinds of quotations, the completion of a proposition by the denial of the contrary, and so on. With that, too, goes the striking style of thought that rests on association and contrast, and often leads from one quotation to another. When Paul says "life", he at once thinks "not death", from "flesh" he comes to the opposite idea of "Spirit", from the "spiritual" man to the "natural", and so on. These things seem strange to one who happens to come to Paul from the literature of ancient philosophy; but anyone who compares Paul's letters with the Talmud will realise that he made very moderate use of the logical technique of his rabbinic school. Reference has already been made (see p. 31) to certain Hellenistic elements of an entirely different kind, in his expository technique.

Taken all in all, however, Paul's way of thinking is not ours. He often tries, in fact, to prove to his readers things of which he has already become certain through their relation to the Christian faith; he pursues this aim passionately right from his starting-point, without looking to the right or left; he draws no conclusions from other lines of thought; his thinking is opportunist, not systematic. Here too, his Jewish inheritance obviously combined with an essential quality of his passionate mind. We may judge in the same way the fact that this first theological thinker of Christianity remained, on the whole, a stranger to the works of Greek philosophy, which later gained so great an influence on Christian theology. He also remained a stranger to the other sphere in which the Greeks enriched the world by creative works of the highest order: plastic art. It was Jewish education in hostility to images, and Jewish strictness in monotheistic thought, which caused him to

Paul the Man

pass those works by with indifference, or even to regard them as idolatrous, as we are told with reference to Athens in Acts 17 [16]. Anyone who wants to penetrate into Paul's mind must remember that he has no approach to art, including poetry; and if some parts of his letters have an artistic effect, it is caused by the unconscious creative art of the preacher, who had something that he was "constrained to say", in conjunction with his schooling in Hellenistic eloquence.

In his style, too, his spiritual qualities may have their share, as, for instance, the passionate single-mindedness that he devoted, first to the persecution of the Christians, and then to the winning of salvation through Christ. It is not easy to understand his character, even though his letters give us an insight into his mind such as is not possible with most of the personalities of ancient times. A good deal of what we learn about it can be explained only by his experience of conversion. But when people in Corinth say of him that his letters sound full of strength, but that in person he is unimpressive (2 Cor. 10 [1, 10]), when people complain that no reliance can be placed on his plans for his journeys (2 Cor. 1 [13]; 2 [1]) when we see for ourselves how quickly he changes from severe censure to conciliation (2 Cor. 1 [5–11]), and how self-assertion alternates with self-depreciation (see both letters to the Corinthians, and Rom. 15 [14–19]), we get the impression that sternness and gentleness, heights and depths, are side by side in his character. If, in addition, we take into account the almost constantly emotional nature of his language, and the excitability of his thoughts and feelings, the question arises of itself whether all this cannot be traced back to a highly sensitive nervous constitution. It would arise, even if Paul had not himself

Paul

indicated that he had to struggle with a chronic burden caused by illness.

For it must be supposed that the words of 2 Cor. 12 7 refer to an illness: "And to keep me from being too elated by the abundance of revelations, a thorn was given me in the flesh, a messenger of Satan, to harass me". The first picture suggests a persistent and therefore chronic malady, while the second suggests attacks occurring from time to time. The second passage where Paul speaks of his illness is in Gal. 4 13-15: "You know it was because of a bodily ailment that I preached the gospel to you at first; and though my condition was a trial to you, you did not scorn or despise me, but received me as an angel of God, as Christ Jesus . . . For I bear you witness that, if possible you would have plucked out your eyes and given them to me." The last words are probably only an image, and not an indication of the nature of the illness (migraine affecting the eyes has been suggested). There may, however, be an indication in the word "despise" (or "spit out"). According to popular belief, both in ancient times and now, spitting is an apotropaic rite which gives protection from spirits; and it used to be generally believed that all illness was caused by evil spirits. But there was one malady in particular against which one spat, and which for that very reason was called "the illness that you spit against": epilepsy. Formerly all kinds of spasms were attributed to epilepsy, and accordingly not only Mahomet and Dostoievski, but also Caesar, Peter the Great, and Napoleon were counted among the "great epileptics of world history". Medical judgment about convulsive attacks, however, has in the light of the most recent research, becomes less rigid, especially through the critical question whether one is

Paul the Man

dealing with a real illness—and so with a progressive process—or with a complex of symptoms, a series of isolated attacks that occur because the body is liable to them. In the case of Paul, as far as we can judge, only the latter need be considered; it is probable, therefore, that he suffered from convulsive attacks that occurred at times and did not, generally speaking, impair his efficiency. For the man who wrote those letters at the age of 50 or 60 was not suffering from a progressive illness that weakened his mind as time went on; and anyone who at that age was still undertaking those journeys—often, if not always, on foot (Acts 20 [13]), was no epileptic (and, indeed, in view of what the apostle accomplished, the diagnosis of epilepsy has often been contested). It really will not do to see traces of this illness everywhere in Paul's life; his intellect and personality remained unimpaired. He himself felt that the illness added a heavy burden to his life, and it was only after a revelation by Christ that he submitted to it (2 Cor. 12 [9]). Its constant threat seemed to him to be a counterpoise to the fulness of the revelations that were granted to him. At the same time, we may ask whether there is not, in fact, a connection between the gift of vision that he undoubtedly possessed, and that unstable constitution with which the attacks were connected. Whether his experience of conversion was bound up with one of these attacks, whether that also applies to his defeat in front of his opponents at Corinth, of which we shall hear again (see pp. 136, 137), and whether the hindrances that he experienced in his speaking (2 Cor. 11 [6]) were of a morbid kind, are questions that have been and can be asked. But one must not make the substance of the conversion evaporate into something pathological, or explain away by a medical diagnosis the passionate earnestness with which Paul carried on the struggle at Corinth; for here it is a question of other sides of his personality: his life's concern and his character.

We have already spoken of the passionate nature of that character, of the emotional nature of his thought, and of the co-existence of height and depth in his disposition and self-valuation. The greatness of his passion is matched by his obviously innate activity; both as a Jew and as a Christian he had to try to win and to keep what he had won. That is why some of his letters become real confessions: he must speak out, win supporters for his own perception of truth, and maintain his position against opponents—even if they were merely hypothetical opponents, as in the letter to the Romans. One consequence of this activity is obviously the capacity for quick reaction, which was shown in his behaviour after his conversion, and which he found so painfully lacking in the Corinthians and the Galatians: if I had been in your place, I should have acted long ago (1 Cor. 5^3; Gal. 3^{1-5}; 5^{2-12}). From that came the capacity, which is so important for the missionary, to adapt oneself: "I know how to be abased and I know how to abound" (Phil. 4^{12}). But another of its results is a quicker change of feelings, which are here ranged, not only one after the other, but also side by side: he realised at least as a Christian, that he himself was the bearer of God's special grace, but that he was at the same time the least of the apostles (1 Cor. $15^{9, 10}$). But perhaps the Christian Paul, who was essentially a citizen of two worlds, was now for the first time recognising and affirming what had already been foreshadowed in his own nature: that when a weak mortal is endowed with God's Spirit, it can almost

Paul the Man

rend him in pieces—"as dying, and behold we live" (2 Cor. 6 ^{9})—Paul stressed it so emphatically that we see how dualistic his nature was. What entirely escaped him was the urge to understand the world and himself as an organic unity; he certainly used the image of the body and its different parts, an image that ancient literature often used about that unity, but he applied it just to the Church. His whole being lacks unity, poise, and harmony; and his thought is therefore without system in its form, and without humanism in its content.

That is what Saul-Paul was, and that is what he was made by his mental qualities and his education: a young Jew, schooled in the Law, but knowing more and looking further than did the average future rabbi; a Pharisee, but also a Roman citizen, passionately devoted to the service of God and his Law; ready to convert others and to defend himself. It would be surprising if such a man had adopted a cautiously balanced neutrality, as perhaps his teacher Gamaliel did (Acts 5 ^{34}), in the face of the Christian movement that was rising from quite different social circles: Paul had to take up a position; he did so, and became a persecutor of the Christians.

4

PAUL TURNS TO CHRIST

PAUL is one of those people whose lives have been rent in two by a single event. We speak of his conversion; but in doing so we must not let ourselves be influenced by erroneous ideas connected with the word. Unlike one who kneels at the penitent-form of the Salvation Army, Paul was not "converted" from a life of sin to a life of righteousness; one might rather say that he turned from a religion of righteousness to a religion of the sinner. Nor was he "converted" from a false god to the one true God, but from a wrong way of honouring God to the right way—namely from the persecution of Christians in the name of God to the service of Christ in honour of the same God.

In his Acts of the Apostles, Luke has told of the death of the first Christian martyr, Stephen. The account had been preserved by the Church, and Luke furnished it with a long speech, and added, at the end, a few remarks that were to connect that particular occurrence with the main theme. Here we read that Saul had been present at the stoning of Stephen, and had thought it just (Acts 7 [58]; 8 [1]). Going on from there, Luke introduced the narrative of Saul's conversion by relating that Saul had obtained from the high priest letters to the synagogues

Paul Turns to Christ

at Damascus, authorising him to organise a persecution of the Christians there too (Acts 9 [1]). Paul had already done the same kind of thing in Jerusalem and Judaea (Acts 26 [10, 11]); why it was to Damascus that he was now going, we do not know; he may have had connections with the Jews there; or perhaps the Christians, who were still inside the community of the synagogues there, were a particularly serious danger.

All this is, in its essentials, confirmed by Paul himself: he "persecuted the Church of God" (1 Cor. 15 [9]; Phil. 3 [6]); he was extremely "zealous for the traditions of my fathers" (Gal. 1 [14]). That does not mean that he needed as yet to be a judge; Acts 26 [10], in which Luther's translation speaks of pronouncing judgment, simply means, "when they were killed, I expressed my approval". The critical objections that have been raised against these accounts have little weight. The opinion has been expressed that the sentence "I was still not known by sight to the churches of Christ in Judaea" (Gal. 1 [22]) excludes any persecution of Christians by Paul in Judaea. But it is a naïve assumption that the victims of the persecution must have known personally the man who was carrying it on. It has also been doubted, without adequate reasons, whether the high priest could give Saul such authority; it is true that the high priest and the Sanhedrin had not the right of administering justice in Damascus, but, as the central authority in spiritual matters, they could probably use their influence, and make use of an unofficial emissary, if the chance came to unleash a popular movement inside a foreign Jewish community.

Thus, after allowing for all critical doubts, we have before us a clear picture: Saul-Paul, a pupil of the rabbis and at the same time familiar with the relations existing

Paul

in the dispersion, of a passionate disposition, but concentrating all his passion in zeal for the holy cause, was caught up into the persecution of the Christians in Jerusalem and urged on to acts of cruelty (Acts 26 [10, 11]). The history of religious persecutions can give other examples of such fanaticism in the case of people moved by religious motives. With Saul a leading participant, the persecution spread beyond Jerusalem, and now he himself took the initiative, and travelled with a few companions to Damascus, to continue there the work of holy cruelty. On the way, when he was near his destination, he experienced what is generally known as his conversion. There appeared, enveloped in celestial light, Jesus of Nazareth himself, whose Church he was persecuting, and who now bade him halt; and blindness that lasted some days showed him, according to ancient belief, that his eyes had seen something divine. Whether and how far his illness had any part in this, we cannot estimate; for him the event signified, not the defeat of the body, but the overcoming of Paul the man by Jesus the Christ.

The old story in Acts 9, of which the two other reports in the speeches in chapters 22 and 26 are merely polished rhetorical versions, is told all through in the style of a legend: a pious Jewish Christian in Damascus, Ananias, had been summoned in a vision to go to Saul of Tarsus, who is living with Judas in "the street called Straight" (now Darb-al-Mostakim). Ananias, who at first resists through fear of the persecutor of the Christians, at last obeys, and cures Paul of his blindness. The consequence is not only the baptism of Paul and his admission into the Christian church at Damascus, but also his appearance in an independent capacity as a Christian preacher. The Acts of the Apostles makes him begin by preaching in

Paul Turns to Christ

Damascus directly after his conversion; in the letter to the Galatians, Paul's narrative of the time is more detailed: "But when he who had set me apart before I was born, and had called me through his grace, was pleased to reveal his Son to me, in order that I might preach him among the Gentiles, I did not confer with flesh and blood, nor did I go up to Jerusalem to those who were apostles before me, but I went away into Arabia; and again I returned to Damascus." (Gal. 1 $^{15-17}$). As we are told directly afterwards that the Christians in Judaea praised God, who had made the persecutor a preacher, it seems from his own account too that Paul began his Christian missionary work soon after his conversion. By Arabia he does not mean the desert—as if he had wanted to prepare himself for his calling by living as a hermit—but, what is much more natural in starting from Damascus, the Nabataean kingdom of Arabia. Perhaps he did missionary work there too; in any case, he did so in Damascus.

It was a development of astonishing rapidity, if indeed it was a development at all. It seems as if the elements out of which the Christian missionary was formed had already been hidden in the persecutor of the Christians, and as if the appearance of Christ had caused the upheaval that brought them out. It is no wonder that the Jewish people were indignant at Saul's defection; no wonder that they wanted to do away with him, and that they tried to do so by a *coup de main* in a foreign town. The Acts of the Apostles (9 $^{24, 25}$) has kept only the final scene—Saul's flight over the town wall, as the Jews were having the gates watched. The apostle himself describes it in even greater detail (2 Cor. 11 ^{32}): the ethnarch of the Nabataean king Aretas—a Bedouin sheik, that is—had the town of Damascus (that probably means the gates) watched, and so Paul was able to flee only by being lowered in a basket over the town wall. Unless we adopt the unlikely supposition that Aretas had some authority in Damascus, we shall be doing justice to the two accounts by assuming that the Jews had hired the Bedouin sheik to lie in wait for Saul as the latter passed through one of the gates, and then attack him when the opportunity came.

But the most surprising thing about the development of the Christian apostle is that he at once went on beyond all the necessary qualifications for a Christian preacher, by the freedom and the systematic way in which he took his gospel to the Gentiles. That he did so from the very beginning is no mere supposition; he himself joins together, in the passage quoted above from the letter to the Galatians, his conversion and his mission to the Gentiles. And when he refers to the classical appearances of the risen Lord (by no means all that were known), he is bold enough to add to the apostles' Easter experiences his own vision near Damascus (1 Cor. 15^8), this being obviously the concluding vision; for in the vision that he had received he saw revealed the will of God as to the Christian Church's mission to the Gentiles. The supposition that Paul was converted a second time—from missionary to the Jews to missionary to the Gentiles—is untenable, for he speaks too clearly of one radical conversion (Phil. 3$^{7-11}$). He began the mission to the Gentiles not more than some few weeks or months after that occurrence, and his decisive motive for doing so must have lain in the experience of conversion.

If we would understand this, we must first ask why Paul was a passionate persecutor of the Christians; for it was in the course of that persecution, because of it, and with it, that he broke down. It was not about the

Paul Turns to Christ

religion of the Law, about works, that his doubts first came, and we must not suppose that he underwent Luther's monastic spiritual struggle; on the contrary, his doubts came on the question whether the Christians really were wrong. What did he see in them that was wrong—what was it that roused the anger of Saul the Jew against the Christians, and provoked him to persecute them?

We can only say for certain what it was that he saw later on as a Christian, in the nature of Christianity, that provoked a pious Jew to indignation; but whatever that was, it must have been connected with the recollection of his own former feelings. What gave offence was not the Christians' belief that the Messiah had appeared at all; for that was a matter open to discussion. It was the claim that God's Messiah was sent to them, the Christians—that is, to people who were partly on the fringe of those who observed the Law, and who partly, as *am haaretz* (see p. 24), stood entirely apart from them. Surely God could not have done that. Just as, centuries later, Nietzsche, the prophet of an aristocratic race of men, looked down contemptuously on Christianity as a movement of the rabble, on that "exaltation of the bad, uneducated, oppressed, and sick" (Collected Works, XI, 1924, p. 69), so Paul, the advocate of the Pharisees' ideal, which was also aristocratic, despised those (in the legal sense) uneducated, weak, and common persons (1 Cor. 1 $^{27-28}$). He despised them—and persecuted them. For here he was called on to make a decision. These people's claim to have had God's anointed with them was an insult to the God of Sinai. Either he had given his Law as a revelation of knowledge and truth, so that the blind, the ignorant, and the dead should be taught his will (Rom. 2 ¹⁸⁻²⁰); in that case the Christians must be wrong. Or they were right; and in that case God was quite different from what the Jews believed. The fact that the two conceptions of God were mutually exclusive was first seen and acknowledged, fully and uncompromisingly, by Paul; he could recognise it as no one else could, because he stood at the centre of the religion of the Law, and not at its edge as did the disciples of Jesus. But because he felt that the Christians' claim was an insult to God and a subversion of the Law, he had to set his face against the expansion of the sect, and had to do it by using force, such as was always approved by the rabbis—relying on the example of Phinehas (Numbers 25 ⁸)—in support of righteous zeal.

Now came the sudden change, which he experienced as a breaking in from outside. He did not work his way in a slow struggle to another point of view, but in the middle of his activity on behalf of the old point of view he suddenly felt compelled to stop; his conviction was abruptly reversed, and he knew all at once that the Christians were right. That is precisely how the account reads; only, in the style of a legend, it is turned into a conversation (Acts 9 ⁴⁻⁶): "Saul, Saul, why do you persecute me?" "Who are you, Lord?" "I am Jesus whom you are persecuting." The fact that the change took place in the middle of the persecution explains its sudden and radical nature; the person to whom the call came could do nothing else than devote himself to the service of the cause that he had just been persecuting, and do so with the same zeal that had hitherto driven him to persecute. So he became a Christian and a member, not of the Christian church at Jerusalem, but of a Hellenistic one, which had sprung from the Judaism of the dispersion,

Paul Turns to Christ

was probably bilingual in character, and was in any case not subjected to the direct influence of the disciples of Jesus. But he became still more: he became a missionary, and in a very special way. As a Jew, he had felt certain that God could not have acted as the Christians supposed. Now he was overwhelmingly convinced that God, after all, had so acted, that he had sent the Messiah to those untaught and often unteachable fishermen and tax-collectors from Galilee, whom the Pharisees regarded as lacking in piety and as more or less without the Law. God was therefore not as the strict Jews represented him, salvation was not restricted to the circle of those within the Law—it could be shared by those of the Jewish people who were more or less without the Law. But if it could be shared by them, why not by others without the Law, those outside the Jewish people, the Gentiles? Individual cases of the conversion of Gentiles or proselytes had probably occurred already in Antioch at that time (Acts 11 [20]). Paul, however, recognised it as God's will that the gospel of salvation in Christ should be taken directly and deliberately to the Gentiles; and he saw in the revelation that had been granted to him the obligation to undertake that task. Thus we can understand that two things were revealed to Paul near Damascus at the same time, or about the same time: the recognition, first, that God had in fact freely given his salvation to the despised and persecuted Christians, and secondly, that that salvation was intended expressly for people outside the Law, and therefore for the Gentiles too.

As the author of this change in his life, a change that marks a turning-point in religious history, Paul named the one whom he was to designate in future as his Lord: Jesus Christ. But we have to ask ourselves seriously how far the historical Jesus of Nazareth exercised any influence on his great apostle. That Paul had once met that Jesus can be regarded as unlikely; all the alleged proofs break down. It is a rationalisation to suppose that if the heavenly being whom he saw in the vision had not been known to him in the flesh, he would not have recognised him. The laws of visions, as of dreams, make it quite possible for one to recognise a person thus seen, even without having known him previously during life. When Paul wrote, "Am I not an apostle? . . . have I not seen Jesus our Lord?" (1 Cor. 9 [1]), he was thinking of that vision near Damascus—he would never admit that merely having seen or known the historical Jesus conferred the rights of apostleship. Lastly, the weightiest evidence for or against Paul's acquaintance with Jesus is in 2 Cor. 5 [16], where, in reply to those in Corinth who claimed the authority of their connections with Jerusalem and the first apostles, he wrote these significant words: "From now on, therefore, we regard no one from a human point of view; even though we once regarded Christ from a human point of view, we regard him thus no longer." That was first of all a repudiation of the view of all those who relied on connections, even on personal connections with Jesus. It would be possible to infer from the "we" that Paul himself had had such connections; but we know from other passages that he said quite clearly, in disputing his opponents' claim to advantages that he himself had renounced: "If any other man thinks he has reason for confidence in the flesh, I have more." (Phil. 3 [4]); "Since many boast of worldly things, I too will boast . . . Are they Hebrews? so am I. Are they Israelites? so am I," and so on (2 Cor. 11 [18-22]). We might expect Paul to have written in this

Paul Turns to Christ

passage: "Even if we have known Christ after the flesh, as I also have known him", if he could have written it. It is therefore a psychologically probable inference, although it cannot be conclusively proved, that Paul had never seen in earthly form the one whom he proclaimed; and we can infer from many passages in his letters that his opponents in the churches did not tire of drawing attention to that—as they supposed—weak point, and, on the strength of it, of casting doubt on the genuineness of his apostleship. Paul defended himself by taking his stand entirely on the revelation that he had had: the call that came to him near Damascus was of all possible calls the most certain and direct, for it came from the Lord who had been raised up to God, and was entirely personal to him, Paul. That was more real and more binding than the historical connection with Jesus, of which the others boasted.

It has been of far-reaching importance for the history of the Christian faith that the apostle based his salvation and his apostolic office—though he certainly regarded both of them as worthy of high esteem in themselves—so largely on his experience of the heavenly Lord; that is one of the ways in which we can connect him with Augustine and Luther. But we may ask whether, in spite of that, it may be said that the historical life of Jesus had any effect on him. That Paul probably entered into verbal duels with those whom he was persecuting, and that the question of the guilt or innocence of Jesus, and consequently his life and teaching, were discussed, is a modern idea resting on all too easy suppositions. If the Christian Church represented an insult to God, there could have been for Paul only one duty: to exterminate it. He would not have entered into discussion with those un-

Paul

learned and despised Galileans; and if he had had any discussion with a man like Stephen, it would have concerned the coming salvation and the resurrection, not the paltry, trifling incidents—which would have been insulting to a Messiah—in the life of Jesus. But that collection of people forming the Christian Church, contemptible in the eyes of Paul the Pharisee, and bringing him, first to a policy of persecution and then to a radical change of outlook, was the result of the life's work of Jesus. It was the tax-collectors and sinners, the weary and heavy laden, that his gospel called to fellowship with God; and it was they who formed the core of the first church. The conviction that God could not call those people gave wings to the zeal of Saul the persecutor; the realisation that God had, after all, sent them his salvation, changed the Pharisee into the first Christian theologian. The most vital link between Jesus and Paul is this: the essence of Jesus' gospel was found in the nature of his Church; and the nature of that Church compelled Paul to realise beyond doubt that what leads men to God is not their pious deeds, but only divine grace and human readiness to receive it.

This message, which Paul extolled in enthusiastic words and defended in theological theses, he called the gospel that he preached; he said of it (and we saw how right he was) that he owed it, not to men, but to the revelation of Jesus Christ (Gal. 1 ^{12}). It was only an apparent contradiction when Paul took his stand on the Church's traditions, which he claimed to have received and handed on to his churches; this concerns the Last Supper (1 Cor. 11 $^{23-25}$) as well as the proclamation of the death and resurrection of Jesus (1 Cor. 15 $^{3-5}$) and also probably the words of Jesus in 1 Cor. 7 ^{10}; 9 ^{14}; and

Paul Turns to Christ

1 Thess. 4 $^{15,\ 16,}$ besides as we may suppose, a number of other such quotations which are more difficult for us to recognise, or which are in letters that have been lost. That Paul was dependent in this sense on the traditions of the Church need cause no surprise; the new Christian and future missionary would have such things handed on to him as necessary for his membership of the Church and for his equipment as a missionary. But all that, however plentiful it may have been, relates only to his material; the Christian must know on what occurrences his belief is based, the missionary, what events he is to relate. The inferences to be drawn from these traditions for the faith and conduct of men are the essential things that form the gospel that Paul claimed as his own, and whose independence of all human doctrine he asserted. He particularly stressed that independence in relation to the first apostles in Jerusalem (Gal. 1 ^{17}, see p. 126), and he had a right to do so; for he had become, not a Jerusalem Christian, but a Hellenistic one, in Damascus, "Arabia", and later Antioch and Tarsus; the historical traditions that he quotes do not sound like translations, but were probably transmitted in Greek from the first. He did not go back to Jerusalem till three years after his conversion, "to visit Cephas" and Jesus' brother James; his stay lasted a fortnight, and was concealed from public knowledge (we must believe Paul's account in Gal. 1 ^{19} rather than that of Acts 9 $^{28,\ 29}$); otherwise the Jews would have wreaked vengeance on him. According to Gal. 2 ^{1}, it was fourteen years before he appeared in Jerusalem again to take part in that most important conference of the apostles, which has come to be known as the Council at Jerusalem. But on that occasion he came as the representative of the Church of

the Gentiles, as a missionary and teacher, and he had nothing more to learn from Jerusalem.

With regard to the intervals of fourteen and three years just mentioned, it must be kept in mind that the ancient method of calculation includes the first year, and that we should therefore say, in the fourteenth and in the third year. The time between the apostles' conference and the conversion of Paul would accordingly be, not fourteen plus three years, but fifteen or sixteen; and this information from Paul is important chronologically. It will be mentioned later (see p. 79) that the only firm basis for such a calculation is the proconsular year of Gallio, before whom Paul was brought (Acts 18 [12]), and who was proconsul of Achaia from the middle of 51 to 52 (or, less probably, from 52 to 53). Paul had then been working in Corinth for 18 months (Acts 18 [11]), and had therefore gone to Corinth at the beginning of 50 (or 51?). From six months to a year should be allowed for the journeys described in Acts 15–17, so the apostles' conference might fall in the year 49 (or 50?). The date of Paul's conversion could therefore be put fifteen or sixteen years earlier, that is between 33 and 35. Jesus' ministry falls in the period between 27 and 34, and his death probably between 30 and 33. From that point of view too, the calculation about Paul seems to be correct. (For more detail, see Dibelius: "Jesus", Göschen Collection, No. 1130, pp. 43 f.). It is satisfactory that such unofficial proceedings as Paul's journeys, of which no dates according to the imperial reckoning were given in any chronicle or written record, can be reckoned chronologically with tolerable certainty.

Our sources, indeed, give us nothing to report about the first ten years that Paul spent as a Christian, except

Paul Turns to Christ

the escape from Damascus and the visit to Jerusalem. According to a definite assertion in the letter to the Galatians (1 [21]), he was not in Jerusalem again between the first meeting with Peter and the apostles' conference, but in Syria and Cilicia. In that very general indication, all the emphasis is on negation; he was not in Jerusalem, but in the northern countries of Syria and Asia Minor. We may take it as certain, from Acts 13 and 14, that in those years he visited not only Cilicia, but also Cyprus, Pamphylia, Lycaonia, and Pisidia, as Luke had excellent material available about those particular journeys. An actual contradiction of what Paul himself tells us is found in the remark casually made in Acts (11 [30], 12 [25]), that Paul had again been in Jerusalem before the apostles' conference, to hand over to the Christian church there the proceeds of a collection. This information is therefore at least in the wrong place; it will be seen later (p. 95) that Luke's references to the undertaking of the collection are nothing more than incidental allusions.

Apart from this remark, Luke relates nothing at all about Paul from the decade about 35–45; except the story of his conversion, which had been preserved by the churches, he obviously had no material relating to him; it was not till the great missionary journeys that he had ample material at his disposal. But if we know nothing about the public side of the beginning of Paul's missionary work, his letters allow us at least to reconstruct his mental state. The letters that we have are only from about the last fifteen years of his working life, from 50 onward; and it can therefore be taken as unlikely that any essential change in his philosophy took place in those later years. Except for changes in the emphasis of certain particular doctrines, all the attempts of scholars to distinguish between a doctrinal system that was as yet undeveloped—in the earliest letters that we have (to Thessalonica)—and that of the four principal letters (to Corinth, Galatia, and Rome), have broken down. Paul himself seems to know nothing whatever of any development of that kind, and we have already seen that he had a right to say that the realisation of certain fundamental things was a direct result of the decisive break in his life.

From this starting-point, in fact, we can be clear about some important basic ideas of his gospel. He himself felt that that break was not a psychological occurrence, but an intervention by the same God whom he had hitherto served. The idea of the great heretic Marcion of the second century, that the Christian God was a new and strange god, was worlds away from Paul: "When he who had set me apart before I was born, and had called me through his grace, was pleased to reveal his Son to me . . ." (Gal. 1 [15-16])—that was his experience. The God whom he had served as a Pharisee and as a persecutor of the Christians was the one who had made his Son Jesus appear to him in heavenly glory. The most expressive witness of what took place inwardly is given in 2 Cor. 4 [6]; "For it is the God who said, 'Let light shine out of darkness' who has shone in our hearts to give the light of the knowledge of the glory of God in the face of Christ." The God who, as the Bible's first page tells, created the light of the world, bestowed that new light too. If that had not been so, Paul would not have acknowledged it at all; the question whether he should repudiate the Old Testament and its God was one that never even occurred to him. He knew, beyond all need

Paul Turns to Christ

of proof, that that God had led him through error to truth—that is to say the God of the Law had revealed to him Jesus as the Christ.

That decision was vital. Paul probably made it without any inward struggle, for it came to him as a matter of course. He could not suspect that he stood at a turning-point in world history, or how far the way of Christianity was being determined by his personal decision. For its consequence was the adoption of the Old Testament by the Church; and that meant that the Christian faith in God was established on the lines of moral monotheism, and that it was founded on certain definite historical facts. It meant, further, that unsolved questions arose about the Law and the gospel—questions which bore fruit, but which also led to dissensions. It meant, finally, that the Church was burdened with the details of the Jewish Law, above all with its ritual (one has only to think of circumcision, sacrifices, or the sabbath)—the Law which had become just as much a part of the Bible as the ten commandments, but which, contrary to the latter, was later to be explained as having ceased to be binding. On the other hand, the moral precepts of both Law and Prophets provided the new religion with a foundation of material ethics, on which it could develop its own morality, from the discussions of Jesus' Sermon on the Mount to the use made of it in Luther's Catechisms.

Paul scarcely suspected all this. For him, questions of moral conduct did not come first. For him, as indeed for all Christians of that time, the realisation that the Messiah had already appeared in Jesus was bound up with the belief that this Messiah—in Greek, the Christ—would soon come back to judge the world and establish his kingdom. That belief in the early coming of the "last things"—the eschatological belief—meant that the whole of life was regarded from the point of view of the end: this life was only an intermediate state, and what was to be done in church, the mission, family, politics, and business, was to be done "until he comes" (1 Cor. 11 [26]). The Christian was living in this world as a citizen of the world to come. Though this conviction unites the apostle with all other Christians, yet he drew his conclusions from it with a thoroughness and an intensity to which the disciples of Jesus had never attained. For him, therefore, earthly connections, even connections with the historical Jesus, were no longer of any account (2 Cor. 5 [16]); his view of the heavenly Lord, who was soon to be Lord on earth too, upset all the values of the things of the old world. Since the coming of Christ, even this restricted life, with its conditions to which the Christian must remain subject, had been so vitally affected by the world to come that the latter illuminated all the dark places of the present existence: "We rejoice in our sufferings" (Rom. 5 [3]). True, a Christian knows that the sufferings of this present time are not to be compared with the glory that is to come; but he feels at the same time that God, through his Spirit, is helping him here and now in his weakness (both these thoughts are in Rom. 8 [18, 26]). So Paul—and he supposed the same thing to be more or less true of every Christian—not only got over the contrast between the grace that came to him from on high and the afflictions of this world, but affirmed that contrast with a feeling of exaltation, because the darkness of the one hemisphere was to some extent a guarantee of the light of the other. Perhaps it is here that Paul's way of thinking in contrasts is most strongly shown; the

Paul Turns to Christ

weaker the human Paul is—undistinguished in appearance, unimpressive in speech, stricken by illness, persecuted by his own countrymen—the more certain it is that all the strength that goes out from him is God's strength and not man's; that is why he has "this treasure in earthen vessels" (2 Cor. 4:7). So we see why he can hardly express himself strongly enough in the description of his life in the midst of death: "For I think that God has exhibited us apostles as last of all, like men sentenced to death, because we have become a spectacle to the world, to angels and to men . . . We have become, and are now, as the refuse of the world, the offscouring of all things" (1 Cor. 4:9, 13).

Thus he was given repeated confirmation of the truth against which he had once struggled so hard: that the disciples of the Messiah on earth were a poor, unesteemed, despised flock. But the greatest shock that that realisation gave him was in its negative side: he could not help seeing that with the best will in the world to serve God, one can pass him by. That was what had happened to him—in his zeal for the Law, in his devotion to the God of the Law, he had become a persecutor of the Christians, and had almost come to ruin. That was what was happening now to his own people, the Jews: with the most upright zeal for the service of the true God, they missed the salvation that that God had sent them. For Paul never speaks of Christ's having been condemned by criminal apostate Jews; on the contrary, it was the logically minded representatives of the religion of the Law "who killed both the Lord Jesus and the prophets" (1 Thess. 2:15).

But now the great question arises: what kind of god is it who allows his people to go permanently astray,

Paul

and who almost sends his most devoted worshipper to destruction? Twice in the letter to the Romans (3 [5], 9 [14]) Paul is not afraid to ask outright: Is not God unrighteous? Is it right for him to go on being angry, if he himself deludes people so? Paul sees himself faced with a tremendous paradox; but having been overcome by Christ, he has already affirmed his answer in faith. But the passionate thinker is not content with an affirmation made in faith; he sees at once that he is at the beginning of a theological consideration of sin and salvation—a consideration that must be carried to its conclusion, because it was a profound emotional shock that gave the impulse to the thought. The question: How could God act like that? becomes the starting-point of his thought as a Christian; and his theology is, in its essential features, theodicy—justification of God.

But—and this is as clear as it is surprising—in spite of that emotional shock, Paul felt that the new life that had risen in him was blessedness. Certainly he lived, like all his fellow-Christians, in the hope of the future kingdom of God in all its glory; but he speaks repeatedly of the riches of the present: "[Nothing] will [ever] be able to separate us from the love of God in Christ Jesus our Lord"; "I can do all things in him who strengthens me"; "If any one is in Christ, he is a new creation"; "For the sake of Christ, then, I am content with weaknesses, insults, hardships, persecutions, and calamities; for when I am weak, then I am strong." (Rom. 8 [38, 39]; Phil. 4 [13]; 2 Cor. 5 [17]; 12 [10]). In his letters to the Church, he often uses, in describing the new state of things, a word by which Christians often described their particular experiences and powers: Spirit. He reminds the Galatians (3 [5]) of him "who supplies the Spirit to you and works miracles among you"; and in exhorting the Romans, he says (8 15), "For you did not receive the spirit of slavery to fall back into fear; but you have received the spirit of sonship." But his favourite word, when speaking of the new being, is simply "Christ". The fact that, when all is said, he means the same thing by "Spirit" and "Christ" is shown when, in Rom. 8 9, 10, he interrupts the thought "if the Spirit of God really dwells in you", and resumes it with the words "But if Christ is in you". That means that he is thinking, not of the historical Jesus or of the coming Messiah, but of the present Christ, whom God has raised to be Lord of the Church, and whom at the same time the individual believer can feel to be close to him as Lord of his life.

But it is characteristic of the way in which, as has been pointed out above, Paul thinks in contrasts (p. 40), that he cannot speak even of Christ without thinking of the opposite: for him Christ is gain, and now he counts everything else for loss (Phil. 3 7, 8). When he speaks of salvation's resting on faith in Christ, the thought "not on works" comes in as a matter of course. The convert's uncompromising outlook is maintained: everything that belongs to the old being is of no account; all the stars that used to light the way are regarded as having set—either they were delusive, or their value was only temporary. How was it possible for them to give any light at all? Here again, Paul is at the starting-point of a series of theological ideas, and we feel that he had to solve the problem of the Law, not because he clung to it, as a Jew, with reverential piety, but because the question: What was God's real purpose with the Law? left him, and could leave him, no peace; what was at stake was not the prestige of a people, but the righteousness of

God. It is impossible to understand Paul's doctrine of the Law unless one keeps in mind that decisive motive; theology is once more theodicy, justification of God.

In any case, the Law belongs to the old world, for God has made it obsolete by sending his Son to those who were outside the Law. Having safely reached the shore of a new world, Paul looks out at the old world that he has abandoned, and, following his way of thinking in contrasts, attributes to it everything that contrasts with the nature of the new. If the new world can be characterised by the word "Spirit", the word that applies to the old one is "flesh". By that, Paul understands not only the natural life with all its associations, but also the world of sinful impulses ruling the body—it has different meanings in different connections. "From now on . . . we regard no one from a human point of view" (2 Cor. 5 [16]) means "we completely abandon all reliance on human relationships". But besides this, anyone who presumes to boast of his position before God, of his standing as a Pharisee, and of his works under the Law, has "confidence in the flesh" (Phil. 3 [4]). So we come to the surprising fact that, in this backward gaze, Paul condemns both sin and the piety that consists in following the Law, as being in the same category. "While we were living in the flesh" (Rom. 7 [5]) can refer equally to a sinful and to a self-righteous past.

Though some theories may not have been developed by the apostle till later, these ideas, these contrasts, and these questions about God and his righteousness certainly seem to have been part of his Christianity from the very beginning. There were two ways of mastering them; one was by thought, and it led to theology; the other was by action, and it led to the mission.

5

THE MISSION

As we have seen, Paul was convinced, not only that the voice of Christ had called him personally, but also that, through the special circumstances of the call, the mission to the Gentiles had been revealed as God's will. The Acts of the Apostles expresses this inward experience by a vision in the temple—a vision that expressly directed Paul, when he was visiting Jerusalem for the first time after his conversion, to the Gentile world (22^{17-21}). The apostle's own evidence makes it impossible to regard this vision in the temple as a second conversion, i.e., from a Jewish to a Gentile mission (see p. 50). The way in which it is used in Acts (it really forms the end of a speech, but is not mentioned in the actual account of the conversion) at least shows that it was not of primary importance in his life. The decisive motive forces behind the mission to the Gentiles were in the experience of the conversion itself: God had revealed his Son in him, that he might preach him among the Gentiles (Gal. 1^{16}).

From that time on, Paul felt that he was the apostle to the Gentiles: "I am under obligation both to Greeks and to barbarians, both to the wise and to the foolish"; "because of the grace given me by God to be a minister of Christ Jesus to the Gentiles"; "For necessity is laid upon me. Woe to me if I do not preach the gospel"

(Rom. 1^{14}; 15$^{15-16}$; 1 Cor. 9^{16}). God had ordained two things at the same time: "All this is from God, who through Christ reconciled us to himself and gave us the ministry of reconciliation . . . So we are ambassadors for Christ, God making his appeal through us. We beseech you on behalf of Christ, be reconciled to God." (2 Cor. 5$^{18,\,20}$). As the end and the Lord's return seemed to be imminent, that service had to be performed quickly: the missionary to the Gentiles had to strive at least to offer salvation to as many peoples as possible; the inhabited world (the so-called *oecumene*), which for Paul meant particularly the countries round the Mediterranean Sea, should have the chance of hearing the gospel message.

That explains the apostle's missionary technique and plan. In carrying out that plan, he would not stop short of preaching through a whole province, city by city, persevering on difficult ground, and repeatedly trying afresh, with a constancy that would be commendable in any missionary, to overcome the slothfulness of human hearts. To do otherwise would have seemed to him to be disobeying God's command. His passionate devotion to the work—the same characteristic had appeared before, in the persecution of the Christians—urged him on. He himself was content to conduct his mission in a few towns, most of which were communication centres; from there the gospel was carried further afield by others, and the apostle went on, often after only a short stay, to the next place where he was to work. Even when he stayed in one city for months at a time, as in Corinth, it was not he who organised and managed the church—a chance remark in 1 Cor. 1$^{14,\,16}$ shows us that even in Corinth the only people he baptised, except for two men, were one family. In large towns all his time

The Mission

was probably taken up by preaching. They should not be able to say, in the day of judgment, that they had not heard the gospel—no, the whole world should hear it.

He planned his mission accordingly. He tackled one province after another, though, in fact, the sequence and nature of his repeated visits were often enough determined less by his plans than by the circumstances in which he found himself. As we read Acts, we are in the habit of talking about Paul's journeys; but we can easily let that give us a false picture, as if the apostle had always been on the move. Although his belief that the end was approaching meant that time was a vital factor, he saw the possibility of fruitful and unmolested work as a charge from God, who bade him stay and work on—again Corinth is an example (Acts 18 [9, 10]). Generally speaking, Paul's activity was based on certain centres, from which he undertook his longer and shorter journeys, and which in the course of years were transferred from one province to another.

The first centre in the journeys was obviously Damascus, if we may assume that those two or three years mentioned in Gal. 1 [18] were filled, not merely with his own reflections, but also with activity. In view of his capacity for quick reaction (see p. 44), this is a fairly safe assumption for the period soon after his conversion. In that case he would have begun, in the second half of the thirties, with the mission in the Nabataean kingdom, and perhaps also in the towns of the so-called Decapolis (Gadara, Hippos, etc.). This period ended with a persecution by the Jews, and the flight over the town wall (see p. 50).

The centre in which Paul settled after his visit to Jerusalem seems to have been Tarsus; we can infer this from the mention of the city in Acts 9 [30], 11 [25], and of Cilicia in Galatians 1 [21]. It is also credible on psychological grounds: he worked first in Damascus, that is to say where he was received into the Christian community, and in the district that was accessible from there; but when the Jews, with the help of the Arabian ethnarch, made it impossible for him to appear in public any more, he went to his native town. We do not know in detail what he did there (perhaps after the year 40), or how long he worked. Luke tells us nothing about it, for that piece of missionary work was, for him, outside the way of world history that the gospel had taken from Jerusalem to Rome, the way of divine guidance and direction that he set out to describe. The inference, however, that this period, with which we are unfamiliar, was full of stirring events, can be drawn from the recital of tribulations and persecutions that Paul himself gives in 2 Cor. 11: "Five times I have received at the hands of the Jews the forty lashes less one. Three times I have been beaten with rods; once I was stoned. Three times I have been shipwrecked; a night and a day I have been adrift at sea." Only a little of all this is given in Acts, and some of the events may well fall in this second period of the mission. It ended, however, not in renewed persecution, but in Paul's being brought to Antioch in Syria, the town where in the very early days Christianity had been taken from Jerusalem and established (see p. 27).

With that the apostle's work, which he had hitherto undertaken on his own responsibility in obedience to God's command, merged in what may be called the official missionary work of the Christian Church. The man who brought Paul to Antioch was Barnabas, who was

The Mission

a Levite and so in some way connected with worship in the temple; according to Acts 4 [36] he was living in Jerusalem, but at the same time he was a Hellenistic Jew, born in Cyprus, and thus not unlike Paul in possessing a second homeland. According to Luke, he had already undertaken in Jerusalem to mediate between Paul and the first apostles (Acts 9 [27]); and now in Antioch it was obviously he who built the bridge between the two missions, the Pauline and the Antiochian. The latter had meanwhile developed along lines which, by the standards of Jerusalem, were substantially freer, and, according to Acts 11 [20], included the conversion of Gentiles. That can well be believed of a bilingual town which even today is still there as Antakia, situated on a linguistic frontier and in a political storm-centre, the Gulf of Alexandretta, and suggesting, in its ruins, something of its size and importance as the third city of the empire; to its community of Hellenistic Jews there belonged not only actual proselytes, Jewish converts of Gentile origin, but also "God-fearing Gentiles", uncircumcised attenders of the synagogue (see p.21). When these people were gripped by Christian preaching, it was not difficult to bring an occasional one over into the Gentile mission. But now there came into the work the man who advocated on principle the conversion of the Gentiles—Paul with his passionately uncompromising attitude. Antioch now became the centre of the mission to the Gentiles, and it also became increasingly what, according to Acts, it had already been: the meeting-place of specially gifted Christian teachers, whom Luke calls "prophets" (Acts 11 [27], 13 [1]), and whose methods were, in fact, not free from traces of ecstasy. They were descended partly from the Jewish dispersion of the Mediterranean, and by their activity in Antioch they prepared the way for a development of historic importance, to be completed by the work of Paul: Christianity, which had grown up on oriental ground where Aramaic was spoken, now became a religion of the Mediterranean world—that is, of Hellenistic civilisation and of the Roman empire. For it was not from Edessa, in East Syria, but from the Hellenistic city of Antioch in West Syria, that the gospel took its characteristic features. One piece of information in Acts (11 [26]) is significant: it was here in Antioch that believers had first been called Christians. As regards time the remark is in the wrong place, for Paul did not yet know the term "Christian"; nevertheless the connection with Antioch is important, for the term is of Latin coinage, created by people who regarded "Christ" as a proper noun, and no longer as the Greek translation of "Messiah" ("anointed"); this too points to the connection with the west, i.e., with the world of civilisation and the empire.

Antioch was the third centre in the apostle's journeys. On the strength of a revelation, Paul and Barnabas set out for Cyprus, Pamphylia, Pisidia, and Lycaonia. John Mark of Jerusalem, a relative of Barnabas, went with them. The choice of the first stage of the journey was probably determined by Barnabas' connection with his native Cyprus. From Seleucia, the port of Antioch, he went to Salamis in Cyprus, and they both preached in the synagogue there. Going further, they reached Paphos, and went before the proconsul Sergius Paulus; Luke here relates a story that ends with the discomfiture of the Jewish soothsayer at the proconsul's court and the conversion of the Roman; but as nothing is said of baptism and the church, one may ask whether the

The Mission

"conversion" meant anything more than benevolent interest. The travellers then went on into Asia Minor, and in Perga (Pamphylia) they were deserted by Mark, who for some reason went back to Jerusalem. The first place of any considerable size where they stayed to preach was the other and less important Antioch, which is high up in the hills on the border of Pisidia and Phrygia. Here they got as far as actually founding a church composed of people who heard them in the synagogue. It is no wonder that the Jews were up in arms; they acted through some of the principal women of the town, who were attenders at the synagogue, and got their husbands to expel the Christian missionaries. The same kind of thing happened in Iconium and Lystra, towns of Lycaonia: it was always the Jews who persecuted Paul and Barnabas, and even followed in their tracks to incite the people against them and compel them to flee. From Lystra, a remarkable scene is recorded in Acts (14 8–18): after Paul had cured a lame man, the people were thrilled with excitement; they took the Christian missionaries for gods—Paul, the speaker, for Hermes, the herald of the gods, and Barnabas for Zeus, the father of the gods. The priest of the temple of Zeus, which was in front of the town gate, actually brought along oxen for sacrifice, but the missionaries managed to dissuade the people from paying them such blasphemous homage. From Derbe, where they worked with less interference, they went back by the same route to Pamphylia, preached in Perga, and sailed from the port of Attalia direct to Syria. If they had gone on from Derbe, they would have crossed the Taurus Mountains to reach Tarsus. Their turning back agrees with the supposition that Paul had already worked there; he preferred to revisit the new and insecure churches, rather than re-enter the old mission field.

He did travel over it however, when, after the apostles' conference in Jerusalem, he went off on a further journey that took him through Cilicia, Lycaonia, Phrygia, Galatia, and finally Troas to Macedonia and Greece. On this journey he devoted the longest time, eighteen months, to the work at Corinth; and that town, placed between the seas, the modern traffic centre in contrast to the classical Athens, became the apostle's fourth missionary centre. But he did not get there so soon or without serious interruptions. We cannot ascertain the details of the events with any certainty, because Luke's account of the journey is at first very summary, and mostly without any indication of the stopping-places; for he was chiefly concerned to show that it was not Paul's wish, but God's guidance, that now took the apostle to Greece and so opened for the gospel the way to Rome. For Luke it represents one of the really great moments in the apostle's career when he stands on the classical ground of Athens—although he did not actually get as far as founding a church there; for that reason he puts into Paul's mouth the famous speech before the Areopagus (Acts 17 $^{22-31}$) —a speech, which to Luke's mind, represents the model of what a sermon to the Gentiles should be. That is why he speaks, on the outward journey, of repeated interventions by the Spirit (Acts 16 $^{6, 7, 9}$), and does not tell us what form we are to suppose they took, and what Paul's experiences on the journey really were. We therefore have to go to Paul's letters for additional information on essential points.

First of all, there were various preludes and interludes. When Paul and Barnabas came back from the apostle's

The Mission

conference, they seemed to have stayed for some time in Syrian Antioch (Acts 15 [35], compare 15 [36]). It was probably then that there occurred the difference of opinion with Peter about eating with Gentiles—an incident about which Paul speaks in Gal. 2 [11–21], and which, if we are not mistaken, began to bring about the estrangement from Barnabas. The break came when Barnabas wanted to take with them once more his relative Mark, who had previously broken faith and left them. Paul refused, separated from Barnabas and Mark, took Silas Silvanus (and later Timothy from Lystra), and went across the Taurus Mountains into the region of the former journey. Having preached in the south of Asia Minor, he obviously now intended to tackle the west coast, the region of the big Greek towns of Ephesus, Smyrna, and Pergamos. But as they were "forbidden by the Holy Spirit to speak the word in Asia" (that is, on the west coast of Asia Minor; Acts 16 [6]), they went through Phrygia and Galatia (that is, through the districts of central Asia Minor), and—we may supplement in this way the intentionally abridged account given in Acts— now preached there in towns of mixed Phrygian and Galatian population, such as Amorium, Pessinus, Orcistus, and Nacolia, which the missionary can hardly have taken into account when he planned his journey. It is certainly possible to understand the name Galatia in such a way as to include the cities where the missionaries had already been in Lycaonia and Phrygia, and according to that, the course of the journey would be different; but if the facts are as has just been suggested, the churches to which the letter to the Galatians was addressed would have been founded in this period. In that case we can suppose from a verse in that letter (4 [13]) that while Paul was on his

Paul

missionary work among the Galatians, he suffered from an attack of his illness (see pp. 42–44), which may have been the sign from God which, according to Luke, meant giving up the intended visit to the coast and making an involuntary stay in central Asia Minor. If, as is possible, difficulties of language made it possible for them to speak to only a part of the population, Paul had to try all the harder to reach a wider sphere of activity in the towns of Bithynia; but again we are told, in Acts 16 [7], "the Spirit of Jesus did not allow them." Thereupon the apostles went, "passing by Mysia"—that obviously means without staying to preach—to Troas on the coast of the Aegean Sea; and there Paul saw (it was the third intervention of divine power) a Macedonian, who said, "Come over into Macedonia and help us" (Acts 16 [9]). As the word "we" comes into the narrative immediately after this, and the company of travellers is obviously increased by one, who then disappears in Philippi, his home therefore probably being in Macedonia, it is possible, but by no means necessary, to connect psychologically the vision by night with the appearance of this companion, who may have been Luke. But one thing now becomes clear: for the Acts, the whole of the journey so far is merely the prelude to Paul's activities in Greece.

For the stay in Macedonia was of only short duration, but rich in results. After the missionaries had travelled quickly via Samothrace to the port of Neapolis (now Kavalla) and from there to Philippi, the first cell of the church, which was to be a flourishing one, was founded there in the house of Lydia, a dealer in purple. The stay ended with a dramatic occurrence, which Luke has kept in the form of a miraculous story (Acts 16 [16–40]). When Paul has cured a girl fortune-teller of her psychical

The Mission

disorder, and by doing so has deprived her masters of her special talent and therefore of the profit that it brought, a general uproar causes the missionaries to be handed over to the authorities, and, after a beating, to be confined in the prison. But there they are proved by an earthquake to be authentic messengers of God, so that the jailer is converted to the gospel, and the frightened magistrates ask them to leave the city. In these graphically described scenes from Acts—it is the most detailed narrative from Paul's missionary work—a new spirit does in fact, for all its simplicity, successfully oppose the customs of the old world: destructively, when it annihilates superstition as well as the girl's illness; constructively, when the jailer is going to commit suicide in despair at the prisoners' supposed flight, but refrains from doing so when he finds that the missionaries, together with all the other prisoners, are still in custody in spite of the open doors; and impressively, when the innocent prisoners refuse to be released secretly, and make the authorities themselves release them.

From Philippi, Paul went with his helpers (but now once more without the author of the "we" of Acts) via Amphipolis and Apollonia to Thessalonica (now Salonica), where he worked only a few weeks, but with great success. Finally the missionaries had to escape by night from an uproar brought about by the Jews. They came to Berea (now Verria), where they had a similar experience, but this time the persecution came, not from the Jewish community on the spot, but from that of Philippi. On the other hand, no church seems to have been founded in Athens; it is true that Acts describes symbolically, in the speech before the Areopagus, the Christian apostle's encounter with the Greek mind, but

Paul

it makes his failure clear (17 ³⁴). So at last Paul reached his real field of work, the missionary centre from which he worked for a year and a half: Corinth. Here all sorts of favourable conditions combined to make for success: the port, where east and west met, where eastern thought was expressed in the Greek language, the city of a vigorous Jewish community and of many "God-fearing Gentiles", a city of seekers and no doubt of many who were lost. Acts (18 ¹⁰) describes the mission's great success, not in a single story, but symbolically in a vision by night: the Lord himself revealed to his servant that he had "many people in this city". On the other hand, Luke gives a good deal of personal information about the time spent there: Aquila (who, like Paul, was a tentmaker) and his wife Priscilla, Jews of the dispersion, who had just had to leave Rome because of the expulsion of the Jews by Claudius, gave him shelter and probably also the opportunity to work and the tools of his trade: for in Corinth he supported himself. Some time after Paul had begun his preaching in the synagogue, a breach came with the Jews, who gradually realised what sort of a man and message they had admitted among them. The apostle went with his preaching to an adjoining house; again we are told the name: Titius Justus, a "God-fearing Gentile", was the owner. Even one of the rulers of the synagogue, Crispus, followed him. It was during this time of his first activity in Corinth that Paul's two letters were written, one soon after the other, to the church in Thessalonica.

At first, the Jewish community seems to have left the missionary work unmolested; the trouble began when "Gallio was proconsul" (Acts 18 ¹²). We do not know why Gallio's taking office gave the opportunity for a

The Mission

Jewish disturbance, but we do know how important this mention of Gallio and his one-year proconsulship is for the chronology of Paul's life (see p. 58). For we possess a letter, which has been made permanent in stone, from the emperor Claudius to the town of Delphi, in which he calls Gallio "my friend and Proconsul of Achaia". The date of that letter can be calculated, as in it the emperor calls himself "acclaimed for the 26th time as emperor". The 26th acclamation falls in the period from the beginning of 52 (or the end of 51) till the 1st August 52, by which date the emperor had his 27th acclamation. The proconsul generally took office in the early summer and remained one year; Gallio's year of office (he was the brother of the philosopher Seneca) was therefore from 51 to 52, or, less probably, a year later. His rebuff to the Jews led to a brawl, in which Sosthenes, the ruler of the synagogue (his is the sixth name mentioned from Corinth), was the chief sufferer. It seems that Paul was able to leave Corinth peacefully, as the proconsul was not inclined to interfere. Priscilla and Aquila went with Paul from the port of Cenchreae first to Ephesus. His destination is perhaps indicated by a remark in Acts 18 [18], if we understand it correctly: that he had his head shaved in Cenchreae, as he had taken a vow. We know (see p. 38) that in his personal life Paul held fast to the religious customs of Judaism, without connecting with them any idea of merit, and without imposing any obligation on his churches to observe them. Thus he had, while he was in Corinth, taken a vow as a Nazirite for a period of dedication during which there should "no razor come upon his head" (Numbers 6 [5]). But that period of dedication had to be ended with a sacrifice at Jerusalem, so it is not surprising that after he had made his first contacts

79

with Ephesus, he sailed to Caesarea and from there made a short journey to Jerusalem, and that Luke reports it all only briefly. Perhaps Paul took with him the first instalment of the collection that was later completed for the Jerusalem Christians; at any rate, he speaks of the undertaking soon afterwards in Gal. 2 [10], as if he had already begun it.

Now he at last set out for Ephesus, in the Roman province of Asia, where he had long since planned to work, and which became his fifth missionary centre. Here he worked for more than two years, though he did not remain in the city all the time, for there was at least one visit to Corinth during this period—a visit on which it seems that a breach almost developed with the church (2 Cor. 2 [1–4]). But a real missionary journey forms only the end of the period; and that is probably why Luke, without a list of the stations and therefore without any continuous source of information, can report little of these two years. The apostle made the outward journey from Antioch through the gates of Cilicia, first going once more to the Galatian churches; then perhaps from Nacolia along the road through Phrygia via Metropolis and through the hill country to Ephesus (Acts 18 [23], 19 [1]). Here too, the quickly formed church had to separate from the Jewish community and its synagogue. Paul now spoke every day in the lecture hall of a certain Tyrannus (possibly a teacher of rhetoric); and we can suppose from the words "from the fifth to the tenth hour", which are perhaps an old manuscript addition to Acts 19 [9], that he had only the joint use of the place during the inconvenient midday hours of 11 till 4. Anything else that Luke reports concerns typical happenings on the fringe of the growing church. Disciples of John the

The Mission

Baptist are mentioned, who obviously considered that they belonged to the Church, without having received Christian baptism, and who now, through Paul, became full Christians. We are further told of acts of healing performed by Paul himself, and of some effected through indirect contact with him by means of articles of clothing. In Ephesus, a city of widespread superstition, there was an even more vigorous outbreak of "pious" veneration of Paul by Jews who used his name with that of Jesus for exorcising evil spirits; but we are also told that, in one case, the sick demoniac reacted indignantly to such misuse, and gave the exorcists a rough handling. Finally we read of the wholesome effects that Paul's preaching had on the centres of superstition in Ephesus, people burning their books about magic, acknowledging their superstitious acts, and joining the church. What he accomplished by speech and letters during that time, and what battles he had to fight out concerning churches elsewhere, we can infer from his letters, which were written during this period to Corinth and Galatia.

In the town itself, too, there was no lack of opposition. The remark in 1 Cor. 15 [32] that Paul had fought, or nearly fought, "with beasts at Ephesus" indicates dire peril, whether we take the expression figuratively or literally. It is also probable that he suffered imprisonment during this period (2 Cor. 1 [8, 9]); and if that is so, there probably came out of it the letter to the Philippians, which gives evidence (especially in 2 [25, 26]) of such close and frequent communication between the place of imprisonment and the town to which the letter was sent, that it can hardly have come from Caesarea or Rome, where he was later imprisoned, and which are a long way from Philippi. Finally, Acts relates that Paul and his work were endangered by a rising of the silversmiths, who made little silver temples for the goddess Artemis (Diana), and felt that their trade was threatened by the success of the Christian mission. Paul himself was not caught in the tumult, but two of his companions were. The town clerk pacified the crowd, and so the whole commotion seems to have passed off without any apparent consequences for the apostles. Nor did Paul have to flee from Ephesus; he left unmolested, having planned to go to Macedonia and Greece. Meanwhile the crisis in Corinth, of which we shall speak later, had been settled by an energetic letter from Paul which was conveyed by Titus; this letter has not been preserved. In Macedonia Paul met Titus, learnt that the quarrel was over, and thereupon went to Corinth himself. Of this last stay in Corinth we know only one thing: that from there he thought out further plans, and announced himself—and his message—to the Romans, with the expressed intention of going on from Rome to Spain. In anticipation of his visit, he sent a mature presentation of his gospel; the letter to the Roman was a letter to a church that he did not yet know. But he already had a number of acquaintances there, for Claudius' decree of expulsion against the Jews had lost its validity, or at any rate its force, and so not only Jews but also Jewish Christians, such as Aquila and Priscilla, went flocking back to Rome. There is therefore no need for surprise at the list of greetings in Rom. 16, nor need it be cut out and made into an independent letter. We do not know what churches Paul visited besides that of Corinth during those three months in Greece, or whether any new ones were established; Acts does not seem to use a list of stations again before the return journey. So we learn at once

The Mission

that he gave up the sea journey by which he had originally planned to go from Corinth direct to Syria, because the Jews were pursuing him, and were perhaps intending to have him murdered on board ship. In Philippi he was joined by the companion (probably Luke) who is included in the "we" of the narrative; he sailed to Troas, where a number of people had gathered who were to travel with him. We can infer from the letters that the churches sent by those envoys the proceeds of the large collection for Jerusalem. Acts gives the names (20 [4]), but, for some reason unknown to us, says nothing about the object, which is mentioned only once later (24 [17]).

From Troas, Luke tells the story according to which Paul helped a young man who had fallen asleep during his sermon and fallen out of a window (20 [7-12]). The sea journey, which Paul began in Assos, south of Troas, is described in Acts evidently from a list of the places visited; the travellers went to Mytilene on the island of Lesbos, and past Samos to Miletus, where Luke makes the apostle take leave of the elders of the neighbouring church of Ephesus, with a presentiment of his martyrdom and in anticipation of what was in store for the Church. Then they went via Cos and Rhodes to Patara, where they embarked for Tyre. As the ship unloaded its cargo there, they spent a week with the Christian community of Tyre, and then reached Ptolemais, from where they went on to Caesarea, and from there, after staying some days in the house of Philip the evangelist (one of the seven named in Acts 6), to Jerusalem. In Tyre, as in Caesarea, there was no lack of prophetic voices warning Paul of imminent danger; that was, in fact, his last missionary journey among the eastern churches. Luke, too, is of that opinion; he has made the speech at Miletus into an epilogue (Acts 20 $^{18-35}$). We must therefore not infer anything to the contrary from the unauthentic second letter to Timothy (chapter 4); Paul never went back to his real mission field of Syria, Asia Minor, and Greece.

6

THE MESSAGE AND THE CHURCHES

PAUL, knowing that he was called to be a missionary to the Gentiles, began his work in almost every town, according to Acts, in the synagogue. Some people have supposed that this is due to a bias of the author, who, they thought, wanted to mediate between Jewish and Gentile Christians, and so made even the great apostle to the Gentiles always begin by knocking at the door of the Jews. That is to overlook the fact that the likeliest audience, even for the missionary to the Gentiles, was to be found at the divine service in the synagogue, where he would meet former pagans who had been converted to Judaism, proselytes, and, above all, the non-Jewish attenders, the so-called "God-fearing Gentiles". These were already convinced that there was one righteous God who ruled history and the world; they believed in the revelation of that God in the Old Testament; and to them, such conceptions as righteousness, sin, and grace, as well as ideas of the final judgment, were no longer strange. It was to them that Paul first turned; and it was among them that, as Acts shows, he found the readiest audience. On the other hand, the real owners of the synagogue, the Jews, adopted (with a few individual exceptions) a reserved or hostile attitude; they soon realised that this new doctrine, although it was propounded by a Jewish scholar, broke open the framework of the traditions of their fathers, and so it was not long before they expelled its bearer, incited the crowds against him, complained about him to the authorities, and even pursued him from one place to another. We can safely generalise from what we are told happened at Lystra, Corinth, and Ephesus (Acts 14 [19]; 18 [6, 12, 13]; 19 [9]).

In relating these incidents, Luke seems, in one respect, to have reduced them to a single pattern, for he lays more stress, as the ancient historians generally did, on the typical and general than on the exceptional and peculiar. Thus we get the impression several times, from his account, that Paul was surprised by the Jews' attitude and then made up his mind, for the first time, to go to the Gentiles. That is the case in Acts 13 [45-48]; 18 [6]; 28 [23-28], in Antioch (Pisidia), Corinth, and Rome; the behaviour of the Jews on each occasion is described quite according to pattern and merely in general terms, and on each occasion Paul declares, as his firm intention, that "from now on" he will go to the Gentiles. The distribution of these scenes over the territories of Asia Minor, Greece, and Italy shows clearly that the author was here concerned with what was typical rather than with single occurrences; he wants to show that it was the Jews' own fault if they remained shut out from salvation. Paul himself knew that his mission was to the Gentiles; but he left to God the destiny of his own people, not without the hope that they would some day be converted (see p. 120). But that was looking forward prophetically to the last days.

We have already seen (see p. 68) that the apostle's belief in the approaching end determined his methods

The Message and the Churches

as a missionary; he did not spend his time on baptising, or, in the main, on what we call organisation. It is true that Acts (14 [23]) traces back to Paul a unified organisation with presbyters (elders) at the head of the Church; but the letters show that the development of the different churches varied according to the circumstances of each. In Corinth, for example, the first convert (Stephanas) put his house at the disposal of the church for common meal; and Paul wanted this family to be granted a certain position of authority. In Philippi, according to Philippians 1, there were *episkopoi* (bishops) and deacons; but they were to be concerned, not with management, but with satisfying material needs. The diversity may be because Paul did not trouble much about those things, but preferred to leave them to others —to the churches or to his missionary helpers. Of the latter we know little except the names—Timothy, Titus, and Silas-Silvanus are the most important. When they are mentioned with Paul in the introductory part of a letter, it does not mean that they have any large intellectual share in it; and above all, we must not let the individual character of certain parts of the letters— parts that have the force of a personal confession—be spoilt by the recollection of the apostle's fellow-workers —not even when he uses "we" in speaking of himself. Perhaps he sometimes dictated his letters to his helpers, but he used the latter especially to visit and care for the churches, when he could not do so himself. He too, when he stayed any considerable time in a town, would no doubt use every opportunity of making a small round of visits, but his main concern would then be preaching, not pastoral care.

Preaching was, in fact, his calling, and with a fine

single-mindedness he made it his life's work, everything else being subordinated to it. When he became aware during his imprisonment (perhaps in Ephesus) that Christian missionaries were cultivating his field of work, so as to supplant him—well, what did it matter, as long as Christ was being preached (Phil. 1 [18])? If he had to accommodate himself to it, so that, to quote the well-known text, "to those under the law I became as one under the law—though not being myself under the law—that I might win those under the law" (1 Cor. 9 [20]), he did so in order to help them all alike to salvation through the gospel. If he often waived the apostolic right to be maintained by the churches, and, as in Corinth, lived with a fellow-craftsman whose tools and materials he could use (see p. 78), it was because he was anxious that he should not be a burden to anyone, and that he should be free from the suspicion of making money out of his preaching. If he was sparing of rhetoric and clever words, it was in order to keep the character of the divine message clear and plain, and unmixed with anything human: "a stumbling-block to Jews and folly to Gentiles, but to those who are called, both Jews and Greeks, Christ the power of God and the wisdom of God" (1 Cor. 1 [23, 24]).

Now, what did he preach, when he began his missionary work in a town? In answering this question, we must not think first of the structure and contents of his letters, for they were intended for people who already believed in Christ. To those who were still to be converted, the apostle had to give both less and more. Less, because his hearers had not yet had access to the theories of Romans and Galatians, nor to the confessions of 2 Corinthians and Philippians. More, for he first had to

The Message and the Churches

give his hearers news of the salvation that had appeared in Christ. In doing so, he certainly handed on the accounts that he himself had received on joining the church at Damascus: "For I delivered to you as of first importance what I also received, that Christ died for our sins in accordance with the scriptures; and that he was buried, and that he rose again the third day according to the scriptures, and that he appeared to Cephas, then to the twelve" (1 Cor. 15 3, 5). But it is equally true that Paul, the passionate and fundamental thinker, did not merely hand on these traditions without any interpretation; the death of Christ for the sins of men, as the Church taught it, needed a firm and intelligible basis; why did it have to take place, and how could it take place? That made it all the more necessary to speak of Christ, though not merely on the traditional lines that told of great and wonderful things in his earthly life. Paul, in fact, saw the Saviour's life not as a human life ruled throughout by God, but as the exact opposite: as a divine life that had come down to humanity; and he was therefore concerned to stress not what was extraordinary in it, but what was human. He does not relate the story of the virgin birth, but says, "When the time had fully come, God sent forth his Son, born of woman . . . , so that we might receive adoption as sons [of God]." He does not describe how Jesus broke the commandment about the sabbath, but he says, "born under the law, to redeem those who were under the law" (Gal. 4 4, 5).

That is also how Paul was able to express the paradox of the life of Christ—a paradox which, as we have seen (see p. 51), had seemed monstrous to him as a Jew, but had become essential to him as a Christian: the fact that God's anointed had come to live among sinners, and had died the death of a criminal. Again and again he stressed how salvation had been brought about in that unique way, which contradicted all human expectation and yet formed the basis of human redemption: God "made him to be sin who knew no sin, so that in him we might become the righteousness of God" (2 Cor. 5 [21]); "Christ redeemed us from the curse of the law, having become a curse for us—for it is written, 'Cursed be every one who hangs on a tree'" (Gal. 3 [13]). But when in this connection Paul speaks of Christ's "poverty", he means, as the context shows, not the absence of money and goods from Jesus' life, but the coming down of the Son of God into the world of men: "though he was rich, yet for your sake he became poor [that is, a mere human being], so that by his poverty you might become [in everlasting life] rich" (2 Cor. 8 [9]). Nor does the famous passage about taking on himself the form of a servant (literally, the form of a slave) refer to Jesus' social status, but to his existence as a human being, which must be called a servant's existence compared to the dignity of the Son of God: "who, though he was in the form of God, did not count equality with God a thing to be grasped, but emptied himself, taking the form of a servant, being born in the likeness of men" (Phil. 2 [6, 7]). It has been usual to describe as the "Christ myth" the whole conception of the early Christ as coming from heaven, not from history; and here the word "myth" is, of course, neither an ancient popular legend nor a modern popular recasting of it, but is meant simply as a narrative that describes the way of a divine being and includes in its framework his historical existence as a human being.

Thus Paul combined his preaching with the Church's tradition, the latter supplying the material, and the

The Message and the Churches

former the understanding of the material. It was only through this message, which he made specially his own, that he preserved the Church from the dangers that were implicit for Gentiles in the Jewish origin of the gospel—which, indeed, was not yet stripped of its Jewish covering. At least one Christian community, that of Jerusalem, was living as a Jewish sect (Acts 24 [5, 14]), being still within the framework of an ancient religion with priests and sacrifices, ordinances and house of instruction; and some, Jews as well as Christians, could believe that all those things belonged to Christianity, simply because they could not imagine a religion without such apparatus. So the question remained open for all Gentiles who became Christians, and even more for those who meantime still belonged to the Jewish synagogue as proselytes or "God-fearing" people (see p. 21); were they to take over the Jewish code with their Christianity, keep the sabbath, become circumcised, avoid the flesh of animals not slaughtered in the orthodox way? Paul answered this question with an emphatic negative. When he was among the Jews again, he complied, as we have seen (p. 38) with certain Jewish regulations, for they still formed the old traditional ordering of the national life among the Jewish people. But he would never have his Gentile churches misled into a new acceptance of those ordinances; that would have been something new to them, which would necessarily have obscured the gospel, and they would certainly have thought that the Christian message could be identified with religion only within that framework. What he took to them was a message of God's grace, and what was needed from man was not efforts of cult and ritual, but only a trustful surrender to that grace.

Paul

On the other hand, there was undeniably a danger that such a radical message might isolate Paul's churches from the others, or at least from the mother church in Jerusalem. Paul did not fail to see that danger, and his preaching continually harked back to ideas and experiences that were common to all Christians. The most important experience was bound up with the word "Spirit". Paul was able simply to take for granted, as regards both his own and the other churches, that every Christian had received the Spirit as a supernatural gift connected with his conversion. "Let me ask you only this: Did you receive the Spirit by works of the law, or by hearing with faith?" he wrote to the Galatians (3 ^{2}). In the same way to the Romans, whom he did not know: "Any one who does not have the Spirit of Christ does not belong to him"—that is, he is no Christian (Rom. 8 ^{9}). There is no doubt that the young Christian churches experienced extraordinary things in their midst: cures and other "mighty works"; ecstatic rapture, especially a beatific stammering of sounds that were unintelligible to other people (they called it "speaking with tongues"); clairvoyance, which could tell what was in other people's minds—"the secrets of his heart are disclosed; and so, falling on his face, he will worship God and declare that God is really among you" (1 Cor. 14 ^{25}). Prayers, too, could be the gift of the Spirit; the old invocation "*Abba*" (Father), which had been taken over from the Aramaic into the Christian Greek, was held by Paul to be the Spirit's confirmation that the person uttering the call was a child of God (Rom. 8 ^{15}, Gal. 4 ^{6}). But Paul clearly emphasised too, that not only wonderful and striking phenomena, but also all the powers of the new life, such as love, kindness, gentleness, and chastity,

The Message and the Churches

were "the fruit of the Spirit" (Gal. 5 ^{22}). Indeed, the gift of guiding the churches, and everything that was done in them in word and deed, doctrine and help, was to him a revelation of the new power that ruled in the churches—the divine Spirit.

Strictly speaking, any commandments that the Law contained about moral conduct should be carried out by Christians by virtue of the Spirit without special regulations (Rom. 8 ^{4}). But those young mission churches still needed instruction to tell them in detail what was to be done, and even more, what was not to be done. To answer those questions adequately, the preachers even before Paul had collected maxims from the wise sayings of Jews and Greeks, and also from the words of Jesus and the experiences of the churches; and Paul shared in the work. That is why certain extracts from some of the letters (Rom. 12 ^{13}; Gal. 5 ^{13}–6 ^{10}; Col. 3 ^{1}–4 ^{6}; 1 Thess. 4 $^{1-12}$; 5 $^{12-22}$) are so similar in form to other early Christian testimonies such as James and 1 Peter; it is the same common material worked into the various writings, to remedy the urgent and widespread need of the newly converted Christians—they certainly knew that they were to do God's will, but they did not know what God's will was.

Baptism was taken for granted by Paul and by all the Christian churches; it had a special interpretation which was often thought to have been invented by him, but which he obviously assumed existed in the church at Rome, to which he was a stranger: that the immersion of the whole body in the water (no other form of baptism was involved) was supposed to represent the descent of Jesus' body into the grave (Rom. 6 ^{4}). As in the mystery cults certain rites were often understood as repetitions of definite occurrences in the myth of the mystery god, and as the partaker of the mystery expected from them a mystical communion with the god, so Christian baptism came to be the bearer of a similar hope. The apostle himself can certainly imagine such a communion even without the ritual: "our old self was crucified with him" he says just after the passage quoted above, and there was no question of any ritualistic copying of the crucifixion; it was the Gnostics who first gave that interpretation to the stretching out of the hands in prayer.

Paul also shows his community with the Church as a whole and the independence of his own thought in his use of the word "faith", a word that begins to show its richness and variety only where a religion of heart and mind grows out beyond national frontiers and where "faith" simply means the conviction to which the religion testifies. "If you confess with your lips that Jesus is Lord and believe in your heart that God raised him from the dead, you will be saved" (Rom. 10^9). That is language that every Christian understands. The fact that Paul moreover ascribed a central importance to faith will be discussed later (see p. 115).

Thus, in spite of the independence of his gospel, Paul brought into membership of the whole Christian body the churches that he founded, and by so doing really created a Church. He united them with the mother church in Jerusalem by that great relief work which he took over at the apostles' conference, and about the performance of which he repeatedly exhorted the Corinthians: the "contribution for the saints" (1 Cor. 16^1, 2 Cor. 8, 9). It seems as if some such financial support had been planned earlier within the church at Antioch in connection with a famine, and that for that

The Message and the Churches

reason Luke did not think of it in his account of the mission, except for the short retrospective allusion in Acts 24 [17]; at any rate, Paul made it one of his special concerns, judging it to be of great importance for the cohesion of the Church (Rom. 15 [25-32])—in fact, he deliberately risked his life in taking it to its destination. The mother church should know that the Christians in the world outside were united to it, and that their apostle was not estranging them from the Jewish Christians in Jerusalem, but was joining them all together in the unity of the Christian Church.

That unity was also helped by the contact that Paul maintained with his churches through his letters. All the nine letters that are here taken to be genuine (see p. 8) were really written to deal with particular events, and were to speak to the recipients in particular circumstances: one, the letter to the Romans, was to announce and introduce Paul to a church that he did not know. He would refuse any human recommendation; he recommended himself with the message that he proclaimed; and that is why, in Rom. 1 [16] – 11 [36], he presented his gospel as a systematic whole. Other letters are polemical, being directed against misrepresentations and perversions of the Christian doctrines (Colossians, Galatians), or against serious misunderstandings (2 Cor.). All the letters were to be read in the assembly of the church for divine service: this fact explains the note of worship that predominates, particularly at the beginning and the end. A good deal in the main part, however, reads like a dialogue in which we have to supply the voice of one of the participants: the church has asked, the apostle answers; or he has heard this or that about it, and now he approves or disapproves or instructs. We get a fairly clear idea of this from a brisk correspondence with the church at Corinth: first, Paul wrote a letter in which one of his remarks was misunderstood (see 1 Cor. 5 ^{9}); then, in answer to a letter from the Corinthians, he cleared the point up, and at the same time discussed a number of questions concerning their conduct as church members. This is our "first letter to the Corinthians"; the other, the first of all, has not been preserved, probably because the church regarded it as superseded, and, as it might be wrongly interpreted, did not lend it to other churches for them to copy it out; so it did not reach a wider circle. Soon after our first letter to the Corinthians, Paul paid a short visit from Ephesus to Corinth, and there he had a clash with part of the church (see p. 80), the consequence being a sharp letter of rebuke and warning from the apostle (2 Cor. 2 $^{3-11}$; 7 $^{8-12}$). We do not possess that either; the Corinthians no doubt took good care not to give it to the other churches to read, especially after the reconciliation had taken place. Its existence is corroborated in what we call the second letter to the Corinthians, in which Paul, looking at the conflict and misunderstandings from a higher point of view, gives the great personal witness of his apostleship. Though, in a long epilogue, he deals with his opponents once more, those last four chapters are not, as has been thought, the older letter (of rebuke) wrongly inserted into this one, for they do not contain things that certainly must have been in the former letter.

We can best learn of the cares of the missionary and the needs of the Church from 1 and 2 Thessalonians and 1 Corinthians; we can trace all kinds of things left over from the old pagan order of society; people still went off with all kinds of disputes to the judge, that is to the unbe-

The Message and the Churches

liever (1 Cor. 6 $^{1-3}$); it was still tolerated that a man should have sexual intercourse with his father's wife—perhaps the slave and sweetheart (1 Cor. 5 $^{1-5}$). Remains of non-Christian piety can also be seen: some had a superstitious misgiving about the flesh of an animal whose other parts had been used for a heathen sacrifice—and any meat sold in the market was open to that suspicion (1 Cor. 8–10). Others confused the preaching of the gospel with all kinds of mystical or philosophical "wisdoms", and accordingly the Christians then called themselves after the alleged founder of their school (1 Cor. 1 ^{12}) after Cephas, or Paul, or Apollos, a Jewish Christian from Alexandria, who had obviously made a great impression in Corinth with the doctrines of the philosophical school of his own town. In that connection, they forgot that no one can lay any other corner stone of the Church than the one on which it is built, Jesus Christ (1 Cor. 3 ^{11}). Others, again, overvalued the ecstatic elements of the new Church life, especially the gift of tongues (see p. 92); they forgot the serious preaching of the cross, so that Paul had to remind them vigorously of the close connection of the Lord's Supper with the Lord's sufferings (1 Cor. 11 $^{17-33}$). But the new Christians too had their worries; the first deaths among their own members caused them particular concern: were those dead people shut out from the kingdom of God, which Christ, returning from heaven, was to bring to the earth (1 Thess. 4 $^{13-18}$)? And if they were to rise again, could the corruptible and decaying body have any further existence in God's kingdom and presence (1 Cor. 15 $^{35-49}$)?

Paul answered those questions. He put it to those who had doubts about a resurrection that there must be a risen body not made of flesh and blood. To those who thought that the most intimate communion with God was to be had by ecstasy, he showed a much safer bridge to eternity, the "more excellent way" (1 Cor. 12 ^{31}): "If I speak in the tongues of men and of angels, but have not love, I am a noisy gong or a clanging cymbal." But he also taught people to face their small anxieties and uncertainties by looking at them from the central point of the gospel; and that is what gives his decisions about matters of only temporary importance their imperishable value. When the "weak" Christians feel uneasy in their consciences through being offered food sacrificed to idols, he warns the others lest through their (greater) knowledge, "this weak man is destroyed, the brother for whom Christ died" (1 Cor. 8 ^{11}). It would be better for them to give up eating meat—and he can point in his own life to the need for such a renunciation, for in Corinth and elsewhere he had made no use of the apostle's right to be supported by the local church, but has lived by the work of his hands and on the occasional free-will offerings of churches, such as that of Philippi, with which he was on particularly intimate terms (1 Cor. 9). But even such gifts he values, not because they help him, but because they show the state of the church's practical Christianity. He himself asks for no help, and so he answers the Philippians, testifying to his pleasure, but avoiding the word "thanks" in a human sense. He himself has moved beyond that kind of relationship: "I have learned, in whatever state I am, to be content. I know how to be abased, and I know how to abound; in any and all circumstances I have learned the secret of facing plenty and hunger, abundance and want. I can do all things in him who strengthens me" (Phil. 4 $^{11-13}$). His judgment about litigation before pagan courts is also characteristic.

The Message and the Churches

First, he reminds the church of what may be called the duty of fellow-members: "Can it be that there is no man among you wise enough to decide between members of the brotherhood?" And only then comes the admonition from the heart of the gospel, in the spirit of Jesus' Sermon on the Mount: "To have lawsuits at all with one another is defeat for you. Why not rather suffer wrong?" (1 Cor. 6 $^{5,\ 7}$). Thus, for Paul's treatment of everyday questions we can take as a motto the passage that he wrote to the Romans, who were discussing the rights and wrongs of vegetarianism on religious grounds (14 $^{7,\ 8}$): "None of us lives to himself, and none of us dies to himself. If we live, we live to the Lord, and if we die, we die to the Lord; so then, whether we live or whether we die, we are the Lord's."

The subjects that the missionary dealt with are many and varied; and so the style of his letters often changes from one section to another. The dialectic, both of the rabbinic method of inference and of popular philosophy with its smooth rhetoric, the conversational tone of personal discussion, the solemn style of his expressions of thanks, the intense style of his confessions of faith, often ending in something like a hymn—Paul's letters contain all that, and it gives them their variety of colour, at least in the Greek text (Luther's translation gives the language a uniformity that has appreciably softened the contrast of colours). We can see that Paul dictated, so close is the written to the spoken word; and that was worth something at a time when writers stuck to conventional forms. The apostle writes instructing, exhorting, confessing, but always from the direct experience of his own life. The emotional character of his thought (see p. 41), which removes him so far from cool philosophical argument, grips and stirs the reader, because he feels the truth of the prophetic witness and the reality of its presence. When Paul's language is like a hymn, he is striving, not after the artistic form, but after the essence of worship; he is a poet, but on his knees; he lifts his voice, but in God's presence.

When he speaks of his own life, his words are borne along by the intense earnestness of his conversion: "If any other man thinks he has reason for confidence in the flesh, I have more: circumcised on the eighth day, of the people of Israel, of the tribe of Benjamin, a Hebrew born of Hebrews; as to the law a Pharisee, as to zeal a persecutor of the church, as to righteousness under the law blameless. But whatever gain I had, I counted as loss for the sake of Christ. Indeed I count everything as loss because of the surpassing worth of knowing Christ Jesus my Lord. For his sake I have suffered the loss of all things, and count them as refuse, in order that I may gain Christ and be found in him" (Phil. 3^{4-9}). But when he proclaims the freedom of the new life, as he came to experience it in the grace of God and the power of the Spirit, he unites with all Christians in a triumphant hymn like a river in flood, into which, characteristically, he does not disdain to bring scriptural evidence (Rom. 8^{31-39}): "What then shall we say to this? If God is for us, who is against us? He who did not spare his own Son, but gave him up for us all, will he not also give us all things with him? Who shall bring any charge against God's elect? It is God who justifies; who is to condemn? Is it Christ Jesus, who died, yes, who was raised from the dead, who is at the right hand of God, who indeed intercedes for us? Who shall separate us from the love of Christ? shall tribulation, or distress, or persecution, or

The Message and the Churches

famine, or nakedness, or peril, or sword? As it is written, 'For thy sake we are being killed all the day long; we are regarded as sheep to be slaughtered.' No, in all these things we are more than conquerors through him who loved us. For I am sure that neither death, nor life, nor angels, nor principalities, nor things present, nor things to come, nor powers, nor height, nor depth, nor anything else in all creation, will be able to separate us from the love of God in Christ Jesus our Lord".

7

PAUL'S WITNESS AND THEOLOGY

It has become clear that, in his letters, Paul speaks to his churches in very different ways. Sometimes he speaks as a teacher, handing on tradition and exhortation, correcting slight or serious abuses, and making the former pagans familiar with the demands of a Christian life lived in this world. Nothing more need be said about that here, for the essential content of his letters is, in fact, something else. In them, Paul witnesses to the new life which is his, and which he wishes likewise to be common to all his readers—that existence which is blessedness in the midst of and in spite of all worldly loss; we have already seen how, here too, he gives rein to his bent for speaking in contrasts (see pp. 40, 62). As both cause and content of this new reality he names Christ the Lord, and he is never tired of emphasising again and again what supreme happiness, freedom, and strength this life "in Christ" bestows, and of proclaiming to Christians, in hymns of praise as well as in the witness of exhortation, the granting of the new life by divine grace. In other parts of the letters, however, Paul starts from questions with which, as we have seen, the paradoxical nature of Christ's life on earth confronts him: the crucified Messiah, the people whom God had chosen and who

Paul's Witness and Theology

had gone astray, the God who accepts sinners and rejects the "righteous"—riddle upon riddle. Paul the thinker tries to solve them; a theologian from his Jewish origins, he uses the ideas and methods of his school, but without proceeding speculatively or thinking for the sake of thinking; his thoughts are not built up symmetrically, but are forced into emotional channels because he is so moved and stirred by the facts as he sees them.

That coexistence of direct prophetic witness and theological dialectic—or, as used to be said, of a mystical and a juridical set of ideas, does not involve any contrast for Paul. He can link them both together (Phil. 3 [9, 10, 11]): "not having a righteousness of my own, based on law, but that which is through faith in Christ, the righteousness from God that depends on faith"—this theological formulation, with the decisive words law, righteousness (of two kinds), and faith, is at once followed by the witness of his own inner life: "that I may know him and the power of his resurrection, and may share his sufferings, becoming like him in his death, that if possible I may attain the resurrection from the dead." We see in the "becoming like him" (that is, in the transformation) and also in the "knowing" (which is to be understood as the perception of the revelation) the mystical and gnostic nature of these experiences. The two lines of thought can be linked together, because they proceed from the same reality, the fact of Christ's life, which released all those forces to which Paul repeatedly testifies, but which also confronts us with the questions with which Paul the theologian had to deal.

If we now think of the first testimony, of the fulness of the possession that Paul is conscious of having gained through Christ, the question arises whether this does not resolve itself into a mystical experience. This question has been put again and again, because Paul uses expressions derived from Hellenistic mysticism, and images reminiscent of the mystery cults; in particular he carries over into his own life Christ's sufferings, death, and resurrection, almost exactly as the member of a mystery cult copied in his ceremonies the myth of his god. Clear as all this is, however, as soon as we look more closely we see that there are qualifications, both in principle and in detail. Regarded as a religious type, Paul is not a mystic. He does not live in the consciousness of the oneness of God and man, which would deny any separation of the two; he sees God as the judge, and man as the accused, and on that assumption he proclaims salvation: "Who shall bring any charge against God's elect? It is God who justifies" (Rom. 8 [33]). A similar situation between God and man is assumed when Paul says that "God was in Christ reconciling the world to himself, not counting their trespasses against them" (2 Cor. 5 [19]); and when in Gal. 3 [22] he emphasises that the promise is given to believers by reason of their faith in Christ, it is further evidence that the people who receive grace are not those who have become mystics by initiation, but those who have that faith. But faith means saying "Yes" to that distant God and to the salvation that he brings about in Christ, and it therefore assumes, not that God and man are one, but that they face each other. The Paul who teaches such things is no mystic, but belongs to the opposite type, which, with Friedrich Heiler, we may call the prophetic; he receives the essential strength of his piety in the consciousness of the separation of God and man.

But when it comes to describing this strength, and the

Paul's Witness and Theology

apostle ventures to talk of his communion with the divine world, he often uses the language of the mystic. In the mysteries the initiate is transformed, through having somehow been enabled to see the deity, into the image of his god; and Paul says that Christians, by beholding the glory of their Lord, are changed into his likeness (2 Cor. 3 [18]); he is thinking there of an inward experience, and therefore not of any act of dedication, nor of any glory imagined in a material sense. In the mysteries, some acts of the cult were understood as representing an occurrence in the myth; and in that way Paul, and perhaps some other Christians before him, understood baptism as representing the burial of Jesus (see p. 93). The inference was then quite unmystically brought into the moral sphere: as Christ was raised to new life, so the Christian was to show himself to be one to whom new life was granted (Rom. 6 [4]). Paul says of that same baptism that through it Christians "have put on Christ" (Gal. 3 [27])—and this passage too can be most easily understood with reference to the rite through which, in the mystery cults, the initiate was made a god by putting on the garment of the god.

That interpretation of baptism with reference to the burial of Jesus already belonged to the mysticism of suffering. The suffering of the Son of God on the cross, an outrageous offence to Paul the Jew, had been greeted by Paul the Christian as the will of God and necessary for salvation. When he himself now had to endure suffering, the idea could not be far from him that it made him more like Christ. His illness, which has already been mentioned (see p. 42), had at first been an unbearable burden, and certainly a hindrance to his work; he had besought the Lord three times that that "messenger of Satan" might leave him alone, and Christ had granted him an answer, a special revelation, whose form, though not whose content, he told the Corinthians: "My grace is sufficient for you, for my power is made perfect in weakness" (2 Cor. 12 [7–9]). He now had the experience that has been known elsewhere in the history of mysticism: it is when the human vessel is frail that any strength is the more certain to seem a divine miracle; so the thing that had at first seemed to him a curse became a means of grace. He learned to understand in a similar way the trials of his apostolic life; he indicated them in 2 Cor. 11 [26]: "in danger from rivers, danger from robbers, danger from my own people, danger from Gentiles, danger in the city, danger in the wilderness, danger at sea, danger from false brethren." He knew that he had to accept all that—want, blows, scourging, imprisonment—as a mark of Christ, that would bring with it an ever-increasing Christianisation of his whole being. But now one feature of this mysticism of suffering becomes apparent which distinguishes it from all the mysticism of cults and contemplation: the union with Christ is achieved, not in celebrating a mystery nor in the secret hour of an inward vision, but in the troubled and dangerous existence of the missionary—the apostolic life is itself his consecration. That is why he can talk of completing in his body "what is lacking in Christ's afflictions", and say that it will be for the benefit of the Church, which was the body of Christ (Col. 1 [24]). Either Paul is thinking there of some kind of vicariousness (what his believers suffer, Christ suffers too), or he means that, till the end comes, a certain number of "sorrows in Christ" are given to all Christians to bear, and that he is helping in the bearing of them.

Paul's Witness and Theology

That judgment about sorrow, however, would not have been such a beatific experience if Paul had not at the same time been given the consciousness of taking part in the resurrection of Christ. Taking part, that is to say, not only in the sense accepted by all Christians, that the resurrection of the one necessarily meant the resurrection of his believers (Phil. 3 ^{11}; Rom. 8 $^{11,\ 17}$); the Christian lives a kind of resurrection-life here and now (the words "the power of his resurrection" were quoted above—see p. 103); and even when he was dealing with the rebellious Corinthians, Paul could take his stand on the strength that derived from the resurrection (2 Cor. 13 ^{4}). Finally, that strength also results in moral reinvigoration (Rom. 6 ^{4})—and here it again becomes clear that the apostle's thought is not, in the end, dominated by the impulses of mysticism.

The same things can be noticed in the phrase that Paul is particularly fond of using to express all the logical consequences of being a Christian: "in Christ Jesus". We can feel the passionate ardour of the wonderful new life when he testifies, "If any one is in Christ, he is a new creation" (2 Cor. 5 ^{17}), and still more personally, "I know how to be abased, and I know how to abound; in any and all circumstances I have learned the secret of facing plenty and hunger, abundance and want. I can do all things in him who strengthens me" (Phil. 4 $^{12,\ 13}$). But he uses the phrase not only about his life's special experiences; he can say of every Christian that he is "in Christ Jesus", and the words "Andronicus and Junias, [who were] in Christ before me" (Rom. 16 ^{7}) simply indicate an earlier entry into the Church—Paul, in fact, still has no word for "Christian" or "Christianity", and therefore has to use words meaning a person's membership of the "body of Christ" (the Church) or his activity in it. Behind that usage there is, of course, no special mystical experience. The converse of the phrase, the idea of "Christ in me", he uses much less often (e.g., Rom. 8 [10]). Once it does seem to become an expression of out-and-out mysticism: "I have been crucified with Christ; it is no longer I who live, but Christ who lives in me" (Gal. 2 [20]); the new life, it seems, leaves no more room at all for the old self, so Christianised is the whole being. But the passage goes on, "and the life I now live in the flesh I live by faith in the Son of God, who loved me and gave himself for me". He is speaking again all at once of the other, the old life; and in that connection what matters is not the union with Christ, but the strength which, leaping all chasms, lays hold of the love of the Son of God—the power of faith.

Again and again we are compelled to realise that just when we think we see Paul on the path of mysticism, a sudden turn or an unexpected choice of words shows that his inward experiences are different from those of the mystic. Nor must we overlook other ways in which his thought differed from real mysticism. For instance, he did not know the mysticism of identity, which makes the partaker of the mystery equal with the godhead— you are I, and I am you. He had too much of the Israelite inheritance, and was too much filled with the Old Testament awe of the eternal God, to be able to put himself, even for a moment, on the same plane as the Lord of the world; and it is probably not by chance, but for the same reason, that he avoids the pagan word, "apotheosis" (deification), although he speaks, in 2 Cor. 3 [18], of the transformation of man into God's image. It is also characteristic of the apostle's quite unmystical relation

Paul's Witness and Theology

to God that he knows nothing of God-mysticism; man can be united with Christ only as with one who has revealed God within humanity. Finally, Paul is separated from real mysticism by the fact that a state of complete blessedness seems to him to be possible only in the future, when Christ reveals himself at the appointed time, to take possession of his kingdom. As regards the present, however, he says, "Not that I have already obtained this or am already perfect; but I press on to make it my own, because Christ Jesus has made me his own" (Phil. 3 ^{12}). When he wants to express the new reality that has been bestowed on him with Christ, he can use the expressions and images of mysticism; but when he wants to consider and understand his own and other Christians' position in the world, he is conscious of the barrier that prevents complete oneness with Christ as long as we are here. He thinks of this world and everything in it as being only preliminary to the next.

Paul's ideas about the end of the world bear, in their main features, the stamp of the Jewish school of theology: first there will come the great rebellion and the appearance of the antichrist; then the Messiah will come from heaven, and the faithful—those still living as well as those awakened from their graves—will be his followers; Christ's reign will begin, and will last till he hands over his sovereignty to the Father. For Paul the Christian, however, that eschatological picture took on a new actuality. The eschatological event has already begun with the resurrection and exaltation of Christ; God has proclaimed his power over death, and, as a pledge of what is to come, has sent the Christians his Spirit, so that they may already be sure of participating in the coming kingdom. At first, the thought of his own death recedes in

Paul

Paul's mind; he hopes to live long enough to see Christ's return (1 Thess. 4 [15, 17]). When he realises that death is not far off, this hope seems to be frustrated, and he laments (2 Cor. 5 [2, 4]) that he may not put on the heavenly garment as soon as death comes, but must expect to be freed from his earthly clothing, and to remain for some time, "naked", in the grave. Elsewhere he indicates that even in this case he hopes "to depart, and [then] be [at once] with Christ" (Phil. 1 [23]); and it does not seem as if this idea came to him only at the end of his life. The apostle's individual hope, always stimulated by the certainty "now we see in a mirror dimly, but then face to face" (1 Cor. 13 [12])—a certainty that really leaves no place for a long rest in the grave—remains unadjusted, side by side with the traditional eschatological picture of the future. He never worked the idea into his theology; he speaks of it in 1 Cor. 15 [51] only as the prophet of a "mystery".

Paul did not work out his theological ideas in great detail, except where his experiences had been so unsettling that they had apparently turned his world of traditional ideas upside down. The crucified Messiah, the discrediting of all piety and righteousness, the changing of the Law from the absolute to the relative, the dethronement of God's people—those were the crushing and almost incomprehensible realities with which he saw himself confronted. That is where his essential ideas begin; they proceed from the realisation that these paradoxes are unshakeable facts; but his thoughts were urged on by the unheard of, indeed the insulting nature of those realities, which again and again confronted Paul the thinker with the question: How could God act like that?

We have seen that the origin of the Christian churches

Paul's Witness and Theology

among lay circles without the Law had made it impossible for Paul the Pharisee to have any connection with them (see p. 51); for if God had shown a preference for those people, then indeed Jewish piety with its belief in the Law would have been put in the wrong. What would be the use then of scrupulously following out all the regulations from getting up till going to bed? What would be the use of laboriously considering how many steps one might walk on the sabbath, when and how one was to separate the firstfruits, on what conditions the tabernacle, in the feast of that name, was adequate—when it was all worth nothing before God? But now God had put the Christians in the right and the pious Jews in the wrong; and the inference from that was that human striving after righteousness, after the state in which God would have mankind—was in vain.

To explain this, Paul sets out his thoughts on sin, which have often been criticised as a "morbid concern over sin", and have often been misunderstood, with too much pious sentiment, as grief over sins committed. Of sins in the plural, sinful acts committed, he speaks when he quotes the Old Testament or the tradition of the churches or conforms to their language; but within the framework of his theological thought he speaks of sin in the singular, and sometimes it sounds as if it were a living being, a tyrant dominating the human race (Rom. 5^{12-21}), or a demon manifesting itself in the human heart (Rom. 7^{7-25}). That is to emphasise the fact that, in man's actual state, there should and must be a distance between God and him, that he is, in a way, infected, so that even his piety, his striving after righteousness, and his knowledge of what is good, turn to evil in him. Paul could not help feeling this as probably no other Jew did, about himself, his people, and the fate of Jesus, who indeed had been delivered over to the Romans, not by the ungodly but by the devout: a mysterious power makes devout people act against God's will; in fact, it almost made Paul himself miss salvation, and it still leads his people astray. This power is sin; and since the time of Adam it has been part of man's endowment—it and its kinsman death. How this tendency to evil came into God's good creation the apostle finds in the story of the fall; about its further development he propounds no theory, but contents himself with laying down the facts as he sees them: "sin came into the world through one man and death through sin, and so death spread to all men because all men sinned" (Rom. 5^{12}). The Church's doctrine of original sin does not come from Paul, but is, on the contrary, an erroneous development and extension of his thought.

Thus Paul speaks from the experience that had repeatedly come to him, that man according to his nature cannot come to God, cannot attain righteousness. And his "morbid concern over sin" calls this indwelling power in human nature "sin". He can even put before his eyes the picture of the man thus tormented by "sin"; it is so close to him that in doing so he can use the word "I", although as a Christian he has already been lifted above this despair, and as a Jew he had not fallen into it, because he did not then think so pessimistically. He says in Rom. 7^{18-20}: "For I know that nothing good dwells within me, that is, in my flesh. I can will what is right, but I cannot do it. For I do not do the good I want, but the evil I do not want is what I do. Now if I do what I do not want, it is no longer I that do it, but sin which dwells within me."

Paul's Witness and Theology

That is the strongest expression of the "morbid concern over sin"; and yet it must not be misunderstood. Certainly, the "righteous" man of every kind is hopelessly discredited; and if ever anyone were again so bold as to appear before God as a pious man, like the Pharisee in Jesus' parable (Luke 18 [11]), Paul would tell him to his face that sin was dwelling in him too. Yet Paul's view of mankind in the mass is not a hopeless one; those words that sound so hopeless do not mention the event that has come to pass in the meantime and brought humanity into a new relation to God—the proclamation of a new righteousness through Jesus Christ. The world and its peoples do not now lie before Paul as a field of ruins, but rather as a cornfield; as with Adam all are subject to death, so with Christ all are to have life (1 Cor. 15 [22]). However critically the apostle thinks of the powers of human nature, he sets his hopes with equal expectancy on the powers of the Spirit—it is only a matter of preparing a way for them through the winning of the many for Christ. His zeal for the mission, the urgent nature of his appeal, and its eschatological form which tries to forestall the coming end, must be considered and judged in relation to that (see p. 68). His "morbid concern over sin" goes down to first principles; but in his practical judgments his missionary hopes come to the front.

It is true that the joy of his mission suffered through the loss of one piece of territory—Judaism; and we now realise even more that the questions about the meaning of the Law and the destiny of God's people belong to that group of ideas that Paul's theology, being theodicy (see p. 66), had to clarify. God's righteousness was, in fact, at stake; he had given the Law, and the Law had proved harmful; it had led the people into a mechanical compliance giving pre-eminence to the demands of cult and ritual.

The Jews had thought to acquire merit before God by following those commandments, and Paul himself had gone to the extreme limit along this way of "righteousness under the law" (Phil. 3⁶). But it had now become clear to him, through his conversion, that the way was wrong, that the Jews, with all their striving after righteousness through the Law, had not achieved righteousness, and that he himself had been taking a wrong course, which could not have led to salvation. Had the Law then been leading him to perdition—was the Law one of the powers of the devil? Or had God himself really wanted to ruin him and reject the chosen people? The apostle fought against those apparently inescapable conclusions with all the passion of a man to whom it was inviolable truth that it was God the Father who had revealed his Son to him (see p. 60), and that God could not be untrue to his promise: "But it is not as though the word of God had failed" (Rom. 9⁶). And to show the impossibility of any such false conclusions, he tried to think out the real significance of the Law, and the real nature of God's way of salvation. It is here that we find the source of Paul's theory of "justification", the theological idea that laid the foundation of the view of salvation accepted by Luther and the Reformaticn generally, and adopted by orthodox Protestantism as an article of faith "with which the Church stands or falls", but on account of which Paul is regarded by many people as an abstruse thinker, remote from reality. There can, however, be no doubt that it is here that the heart of Paul the thinker beats most

Paul's Witness and Theology

vigorously, and that it is here that we have to look for the core of his message. Having already been accustomed, as a Jew, to think of man and the world as created by God, he was bound to put the questions: Why are those without the Law the very people on whom God has bestowed his salvation—why has the Law failed, why had it to fail, as the way of salvation?

The answer given by Paul to these questions, which were so disturbing and far-reaching to a pious Jew, grew out of the beatific experience of the new life that had been given him: "behold, now is the acceptable time; behold, now is the day of salvation" (2 Cor. 6 ^{2}). But that day of salvation had become a reality through God's having sent his Son "when the time had fully come" (Gal. 4 ^{4}), and having given "by his grace . . . the redemption which is in Christ Jesus" (Rom. 3 ^{24}). Till now, Paul had thought with the Jews that man must earn God's approval by obedience to the requirements of the Law, through "works of the law"; but now it had come to him —and he would say the same for all Jewish Christians— that God had shown a totally different way of deliverance: "We ourselves, who are Jews by birth and not Gentile sinners, yet who know that a man is not justified by works of the law but through faith in Jesus Christ, even we have believed in Christ Jesus, in order to be justified by faith in Christ, and not by works of the law" (Gal 2 ^{15}, ^{16}). Man is shown here in an entirely new position before God: he may count on God's approval, not because of any works of his own, but because he can believe in Christ; and just as Paul had been accustomed to use the Jewish ideas of "attaining righteousness" and "works of the law" in describing the relation to God which he now recognised as false, so he uses the same kind of language in describing the new life: "But now the righteousness of God has been manifested apart from law . . . the righteousness of God through faith in Jesus Christ for all who believe . . . since all have sinned . . . they are justified by his grace as a gift, through the redemption which is in Christ Jesus, whom God put forward as an expiation by his blood, to be received by faith. This was to show God's righteousness, because in his divine forbearance he had passed over former sins . . . For we hold that a man is justified by faith apart from works of law" (Rom. 3 $^{21-28}$). If the Christian churches' tradition, which he received when he became a Christian, testified "that Christ died for our sins in accordance with the scriptures" (1 Cor. 15 ^{3}—see p. 89), Paul now realised why that had to be so: it was in that very way, "a stumbling-block to Jews and folly to Gentiles", that God meant to show his love and save the believers (1 Cor. 1 ^{21}, ^{23}).

Later Christian theologians have not always succeeded in stopping at that bold thought, and in not wanting to know further why it was through his Son's atonement that God wanted to show his love; and especially since Anselm of Canterbury (d. 1109) the view has been widespread that Paul here explains exactly why it was only through the death of his Son that God could have provided for the fulfilment both of his requirement that human sin should be punished and of his will that mankind should be saved. Paul knew nothing of all those ideas; he was certain that men are saved from the power of sin and death, by God who allowed Jesus Christ to die; and in testifying to that wonderful happening, he used the ideas with which he was familiar—those of expiatory sacrifice and annihilation of the guilt of sin.

Paul's Witness and Theology

Although the Jews, and Paul with them, had thought that one who died on the cross was cursed by God, he now knew that, on the contrary, God had through that atonement preserved men from the curse that they had incurred as sinners: "Christ redeemed us from the curse of the law, having become a curse for us" (Gal. 3 13). If we of today, who do not include propitiatory sacrifice and religious curse in the realities of our experience, find this language foreign to us, yet we too can feel the prophetic power of the message, when Paul can speak of the same reality, using the idea of reconciliation: "God was in Christ reconciling the world to himself, not counting their trespasses against them, and entrusting to us the message of reconciliation" (2 Cor. 5 19).

That is the commission that Paul, as an apostle, had to carry out after his conversion—to proclaim how God had of his own will re-created man—God, acting with absolute righteousness (all human expectation notwithstanding), in recognising those without the Law as "righteous", in accepting man just as he is, and in creating for him the possibility of salvation. And if man is to accept this message of God's act of reconciliation and justification, only one thing is vital: he must believe— "If you confess with your lips that Jesus is Lord and believe in your heart that God raised him from the dead, you will be saved" (Rom. 10 9). That is what believing means—to look away from self, disregard both one's wretchedness and one's merits, and trust in God's having settled the matter through Jesus Christ. That most certainly means first of all a complete acceptance of the preaching of Christ crucified and risen again, for "faith comes from what is heard, and what is heard comes by the preaching of Christ" (Rom. 10 17). But faith is for

Paul

Paul immeasurably more than that—whoever believes commits himself to God despite all human hope, as Abraham did; indeed whoever believes receives the Spirit from God, and now lives in love (Rom. 4 ^{18}; Gal. 3 ^{2}, 5 ^{6}). Thus faith is not a work of the Law, a human accomplishment with all its doubtfulness and uncertainty; and yet God's working in Jesus Christ reaches man only when he believes: "For we hold that a man is justified by faith apart from works of law" (Rom. 3 ^{28}). But if Paul gives faith a central place, that meant much more than what the Christian tradition had already said about faith (see p. 94); it meant that, in the burning questions that confronted Paul through his conversion, the righteous God was shown to be the author of man's present salvation.

But there were still two questions to be answered: First, what was now the significance of the Law? Secondly, did this new and final revelation mean the rejection of the chosen people? God's calling of those without the Law had shown that man could not become righteous by fulfilling its requirements. Then was the Law evil? Paul was quite convinced that such a conclusion must be rejected: "the law is holy, and the commandment is holy and just and good" (Rom. 7 ^{12}). But as man would have to fulfil, and yet cannot fulfil, all the requirements of the Law, the Law has no longer any power, except to show man how lost he is before God and to sink him deeper and deeper in his helplessness (Rom. 3 ^{20}; 5 ^{20}). Paul was quite clear that behind the breakdown of the Law he could see the working of sin, that demonic power of which we have already spoken (see p. 111): "Did that which is good, then, bring death to me? By no means! It was sin, working death in me

Paul's Witness and Theology

through what is good, in order that sin might be shown to be sin, and through the commandment might become sinful beyond measure" (Rom. 7^{13}). But he was not content with merely seeing the demonic background of man's relation to God; his thought was too profound to rest before it had grasped the will of God behind the riddle: it was none of God's will that men should attain to life through the Law; the Law was to be only like a poor slave or jailer, to make men ready to hear the gospel of Christ (Gal. 3 $^{21-24}$), "For Christ is the end of the law, that every one who has faith may be justified" (Rom. 10 ^{4}). That is how Paul judged as a Christian, and that is how he was bound to judge, because, as a believer, he could see out of his own experience of the new life that the "old covenant" was only the indirect way that God had chosen.

But were not the Jews now rejected—those who were still holding fast to that old covenant, which, after all, had once been God's sole way? Was it not because God had turned away from his chosen people that he called Paul to be an apostle to the Gentiles? Paul put this question with all the passionateness of the pious Jew whose love of his people was so great that he could write to the Romans, "For I could wish that I myself were accursed and cut off from Christ for the sake of my brethren, my kinsmen by race"(9 ^{3}). He did not by any means overlook the unbelief of the majority of the Jews towards the preaching of the gospel; and he knew that it was the pious Jews "who killed both the Lord Jesus and the prophets, and drove us out, and displease God and oppose all men by hindering us from speaking to the Gentiles that they may be saved—so as always to fill up the measure of their sins" (1 Thess, 2 $^{15, 16}$). And yet he began again and again to preach in the synagogues (see p. 85), emphasising that "the gospel...is the power of God for salvation to every one who has faith, to the Jew first and also to the Greek" (Rom. 1¹⁶; compare 1 Cor. 1²⁴). So he did not deny that it was the Jews' own fault if they had shut themselves out from salvation; but at the same time he saw prophetically in that refusal a way round for God (Rom. 11 ¹¹⁻³²)—the Jews were to be made jealous by the conversion of the Gentiles, the calling of a new people of God; and eventually "all Israel will be saved". That was a "mystery" that Paul proclaimed, a prophetic view of the anticipated early end of the world. It has often been thought that he wanted here to make a prediction that would hold good for all time about events in the world's history; but that is erroneous, if for no other reason than that, according to this prophetic view, the end of the world was close at hand. He was rather proclaiming a divine secret, which he had received by a personal revelation and which put an end to his own doubts—the hope that God would still, after all, lead his chosen people, in spite of their refusal, to recognise their true Messiah. On the basis of that hope he preached the more zealously to the Gentiles and called them to the Messiah's Church; in that hope Paul the thinker found rest, and there remained for him only amazement and adoration as he considered the ways of God: "O the depth of the riches and wisdom and knowledge of God! how unsearchable are his judgments and how inscrutable his ways! For from him and through him and to him are all things. To him be glory forever. Amen." (Rom. 11 ³³, ³⁶).

So Paul tried to clear up, by theological reflection, the questions that came to him through his conversion and

Paul's Witness and Theology

through the reality (which he found so surprising at first) of the Messiah's new Church. But he did not ignore the problem of making up his mind about the reality which had been with him on all sides since he had become a Christian, and which needed all his missionary effort to build it up—the Church. We have already seen that, in common with all the Christian churches, he was familiar with baptism as a rite performed on entering the Christian Church, and that he understood the act of baptism—likewise in agreement with the Hellenistic churches—to represent dying with Christ (see p. 93). Whoever accepts baptism as a believer does not experience, according to Paul, an inward death; he does not undergo once more, in some mysterious way, the death of Christ ("The death he died he died to sin, once for all" Rom. 6 [10]), but he does have the experience, in faith, of actually receiving a share in the effect of Christ's death and resurrection, and he is therefore dead to sin and lives for God—in so far as he believes: "and you were buried with him in baptism, in which you were also raised with him through faith in the working of God, who raised him from the dead. And you, who were dead in trespasses . . . , God made alive together with him, having forgiven us all our trespasses" (Col. 2 [12, 13]). According to this, Paul saw in baptism a divine action on human beings, making what God has done in Christ a personal reality to the individual believer, conveying to him at the same time the gift of the Holy Spirit, and so receiving him into the new community of salvation, the "body of Christ": "For by one Spirit we were all baptised into one body" (1 Cor 12 [13]). Thus every single Christian shares in the reality of the one Church, which, being the body of Christ, receives its life from its Head

(Col. 2 ^{19}), and includes the whole of the Christian churches. And just as Paul saw in baptism not merely a rite of admission, but the incomprehensible reality of God's saving action in every baptised person, so membership of the Church of Jesus Christ meant more to him than merely belonging to some religious community: "For as in one body we have many members, and all the members do not have the same function, so we, though many, are one body in Christ, and individually members one of another" (Rom. 12 $^{4,\ 5}$). Christians really have, here and now, a share in the new life that has been brought through Christ; "for in Christ Jesus you are all sons of God, through faith" (Gal. 3 ^{26})—that is, as parts of his body. Again baptism appears as the event that signifies the beginning of this membership of the body of Christ; and it is on the believer that this divine gift is bestowed in baptism.

Just as Paul understood baptism as the initiating act of Church membership, so he understood the Lord's Supper as a continual renewal of that membership. He had taken over this ceremonial procedure too from the custom of the original church in its divine services, which followed Jesus' daily meal-time custom as well as his last meal. He assumed from the beginning that it was the custom in the churches that none but the actual church members could take part in this common meal, while the unbaptised could share only in the service of the word. For baptised Christians, taking part in the Lord's Supper meant continually re-entering into communion with the living Lord of the Church: "The cup of blessing which we bless, is it not a participation in the blood of Christ? The bread which we break, is it not a participation in the body of Christ? Because there is one loaf, we who are

Paul's Witness and Theology

many are one body, for we all partake of the same loaf" (1 Cor. 10 $^{16,\ 17}$). When Christians drink the wine together, Christ's sacrificial death again becomes effective for them; they feel anew that it was for them that Jesus Christ died and rose again, and that they have thereby been freed from the bondage of guilt and death. When they eat together of the same bread, they are joined once more in the body of Christ, the Church, and share anew in its strength. But again, that does not happen simply because the rite is celebrated—Paul had to contend quite early against that misconception (see especially 1 Cor. 10); the essential thing is that the Christian should "[discern] the body" (1 Cor. 11 ^{29})—that is, that he should know that he partakes of the Lord's body, and that he must be and remain in the faith, if the reality of the Lord's Supper is to be a means of blessing for him, and not a judgment (1 Cor. 10 $^{6-12}$; 11 $^{29-31}$).

That, indeed, is the common characteristic of all these theological ideas of Paul—proceeding from the Jewish God of history, he sought to tie the Christian's religious life firmly to God's historical act of salvation in Christ, and to prevent piety from degenerating into mere mysticism, or from being based solely on formal acts of worship. So he confidently proclaimed to his churches what great gifts they had received, and would continue to receive, through baptism and the Lord's Supper. But he could also talk of the death of Christ without mentioning baptism: "we are convinced that one has died for all; therefore all have died" (2 Cor. 5 ^{14}); he could say that it is through faith alone that we receive the Spirit: "Did you receive the Spirit by works of the law, or by hearing with faith?" (Gal. 3 ^{2}); in fact, he could make the new life derive simply from Christ's act, "who

Paul

died for us so that . . . we might live with him" (1 Thess. 5 ¹⁰). He could also make the sharing in the blessings of Christ's body depend entirely on hearing God's call: "And let the peace of Christ rule in your hearts, to which indeed you were called in the one body" (Col. 3 ¹⁵). So he knew that Christians became part of the body of the Church, and he strongly emphasised that their gifts and the Church were in unity, for the sake of which, in fact, he incurred personal danger (see p. 95). But at the same time, in his uncompromising way, he insisted that one's existence as a Christian is due solely and without qualification to God's act in Christ, to which Paul himself owed his new life, and in which he found the solution of the problem that the existence of the Christian Church had set him. So he found an answer to the questions about God's righteousness—questions which had been confronting him, as a devout Pharisee, since his conversion. So he succeeded too—and herein lies the far-reaching importance of his theological thought—in safeguarding the Christian message from the return of Jewish legalism as well as from disintegration into a mere religion of sacraments, because he repeatedly stressed the indissoluble connection between faith and God's act of salvation. That is why Paul the theologian has become the standard by which all Christian thought must be tested.

8

STRUGGLES

PAUL had been led by his conversion to realise that the way by which the Jews hoped to reach God could not lead to the desired end, because God himself, by sending his Son and calling into existence the Christian Church, had shown that way to be wrong. As a trained theologian and a former convinced follower of the legal way, he had recognised quite clearly the contrast between God's newly proclaimed way of salvation and the way of the Law, and had concluded that, with the elimination of the Law, God's salvation was in fact expressly meant for the Gentiles too (see p. 50). But the very fact that, as a Jewish theologian, he had so clearly recognised the natural contrast between the Christian faith and the Jewish religion, and was prepared to draw the logical conclusions, was bound from the first to bring a certain tension into his relation with Jesus' first disciples, who had at the same time become the first leaders of the Christian church in Jerusalem. Those first disciples, among whom Peter played the leading part, were, as we have seen (see p. 27), closely connected with Judaism; they held their meetings partly in the temple (Acts 2 [46]), and, as the story of Cornelius (Acts 10) shows, they were not open to the idea that uncircumcised Gentiles should

Paul

be called into the Christian Church. Now they were the bearers of the traditions of the earthly Jesus and the first witnesses of his resurrection, and for that reason there could be no Christian Church without some sort of connection with this original church. In addition to the latter, however, since the persecution and flight of the Hellenistic Jewish Christians of Jerusalem, whose spokesman had been Stephen, Christian churches had been formed in the Jewish dispersion; and these counted former pagans among their members. When Paul had become a Christian on the way to Damascus, he had joined one of those Hellenistic Christian churches, and had not at first entered into relations with the first apostles in Jerusalem. Whether that was accident or design we cannot tell; in any case the fact is that Paul, according to his own solemn assertion (Gal. 1 $^{17,\ 18}$), stayed away from Jerusalem for two or three years. Moreover, it is plain from certain passages in Galatians (1 $^{1-12}$) that the reason why he could stay away from Jerusalem was that he traced his gospel back solely to the direct call that he had received from the heavenly Lord, so that he needed for his work as apostle no authority, or even instruction, from the first apostles. Then, about three years later (the statements in Acts 9 $^{19-30}$ have to be corrected by Gal. 1 ^{18}), Paul did go to Jerusalem; but he stayed there only a fortnight and talked only to Peter and Jesus' brother James (see p. 57). We do not know what was discussed when they met, so it is no use trying to guess whether Paul talked at that early date with the people of Jerusalem about the validity of the mission to the Gentiles and the question of freedom from the Law; in any case he did not allow the task assigned to him by the Lord —his mission to the Gentiles—to be called in question.

Struggles

We know very little of Paul's missionary activity in the following fourteen years or thereabouts, as the writer of Acts seems to have had no sources of information, and Paul himself mentions nothing except that he worked in Syria and Cilicia (Gal. 1 ^{21}; see pp. 59, 70). No doubt he worked, avowedly as a missionary to the Gentiles, from the two missionary centres of Tarsus and Antioch, and, in particular, through Cyprus and the south of Asia Minor (the first missionary journey of which we have fairly detailed information—Acts 13, 14; see pp. 72, 73), and so founded churches that consisted for the most part of former pagans. He never demanded of those Gentiles that they should take over the Jewish Law, because such a demand would, of course, have meant that the fulfilling of the injunctions of the Law would appear to them, just when they were entering the Christian Church, as a work without which they could not obtain God's approval. Freedom from the Law, no doubt practised to a certain extent by the pre-Pauline Gentile mission of the Hellenistic Jewish Christians, was thus for Paul an intentional and logical policy from the very beginning. He was opposed, however, by the equally logical view of those Jewish Christians at Jerusalem who continued to assert that compliance with the Law was not to be bargained away, but was an essential requirement from anyone who would stand before God. For those Jewish Christians, faith in the risen Jesus Christ did not mean a new religion, but only the recognition of the fact that the Messiah whom the Jews were erroneously still expecting had already done his work on earth in the person of Jesus, and that he would soon return to establish his kingdom.

Those "believers who belonged to the party of the

Paul

Pharisees", as Luke calls them (Acts 15 [5]), obviously did not comprise the whole body of Jewish Christians; Paul distinguished them clearly—calling them "false brethren" (Gal. 2 [4])—from the actual first apostles, the "pillars" James, Peter, and John (Gal. 2 [9]); but he could also say that those false brethren had gained so great an influence in the church at Jerusalem that there was a danger of a break between Pauline Gentile Christianity and the Jerusalem church. For of course reports about Paul's mission to the Gentiles, with its freedom from the Law, had meanwhile reached Jerusalem, and had aroused in the influential extreme wing of the church there not only general indignation, but probably also the fear that in the Pauline churches the Jewish Christians too might be caused to abandon the requirements of the Law (Acts 21 [21]). Indeed, that indignation and fear did not remain merely a state of mind, but turned into action—first and foremost, as far as we can tell, at Antioch in Syria, the centre of the pre-Pauline Gentile mission and then also of the missionary activity of Paul himself, which united with it. Emissaries had been sent there on behalf of the strict legalistic Jews of Jerusalem (the latter have come to be generally known as Judaisers); and those emissaries were to try to enforce the circumcision of Gentiles inside the Christian churches and abolish the freedom that they had hitherto been allowed in relation to the Law (Acts 15 [1, 5]; Gal. 2 [3, 4]). That caused a real danger that the one Church might split into at least two groups, since Paul, from loyalty to the divine commission with which he had been entrusted, could not agree that the Gentiles who had been won for Christ should be made Jews retrospectively, and that an almost insuperable obstacle should thus be put in the way of the

Struggles

free working of the Spirit of Christ among the Gentiles. To avoid such a split, he decided to go to Jerusalem after an absence of about fourteen years, to discuss the matter with the first apostles. He took with him Barnabas, who some fourteen years earlier had built a bridge between Paul and the Jerusalem Christians and had once brought him from Tarsus to Antioch, and Titus, an uncircumcised Gentile Christian.

About this meeting of the apostles, which has come to be known as the Council at Jerusalem, we have only the brief remarks of Paul (Gal. 2 [1-10]) and a detailed report in Acts (15 [1-29]). Although this has been repeatedly contested, it cannot be seriously doubted that the two texts refer to the same event. They contradict each other, however, mainly on one point where it seems hardly possible to reconcile them: whereas Paul solemnly asserts that he did not accept any kind of obligation except that of making a collection for the poor of the Jerusalem church, Acts reports that the assembly decided to impose on Gentile Christians the requirement that they should "abstain from pollution of idols, and from unchastity and from what is strangled [i.e., not slaughtered in the orthodox way], and from [partaking of] blood" (Acts 15 [20]); and that this decision was communicated in a letter sent by delegates to the Christian churches in Antioch, Syria, and Cilicia. Now this statement is in contradiction, not only to Paul's account of the conference, but also to the fact that later, in Galatians and 1 Corinthians, he upheld the complete freedom of Christians from the obligation of following the Law, and, on the question of eating meat offered to idols (1 Cor. 8–10), did not even mention that he had co-operated in reaching a decision which would, of course, have been binding for the Corinthians too.

There must therefore be an error here in the account given in Acts; it is probable that the "apostles' decree" was issued at a later time (certainly without Paul's participation) and had nothing to do with the Council at Jerusalem.

Apart from that, the report in Acts about the Council at Jerusalem shows that Luke had no very accurate knowledge of the details of what had happened there, so that we have to rely almost entirely on Paul's account. Paul had gone to Jerusalem to convince the Christians there by putting before them his view about the mission to Gentiles, namely that compliance with the Judaisers' demand that the Jewish Law should be imposed on Gentile Christians would amount to a denial of the commission that had been entrusted to him by the heavenly Lord himself. It is obvious that the extremists in Jerusalem now tried to have their way by demanding that Titus, the Gentile Christian whom Paul had brought with him, must be circumcised if they were to recognise him as a full member of the Church of Christ the Messiah. Paul was able to prevent that demand from being complied with, as the first apostles themselves took his side, recognised his divine commission, and agreed with him that no compliance with the Jewish Law was to be demanded from Gentiles who became Christians. It was agreed that Paul and Barnabas should carry on the mission among the Gentiles, while the first apostles should devote themselves mainly to winning Jews; and Paul undertook the obligation of organising, in the Gentile Christian churches that he had founded, a collection for the poor of Jerusalem, so as to give expression, by an unmistakable act of goodwill, to the fact that the Gentile Christians too felt that they were united with the original

Struggles

church in Jerusalem. Later on, he strove hard to carry out this obligation faithfully, and in doing so he did not fear to risk his life (see p. 95).

Those agreements seemed to have dispelled the danger that the Gentile Christians might have to give way to the pressure of the uncompromising Jewish Christians, or that the one Church of Jesus Christ, which was composed of Jews and Gentiles, might split in two. How far they still were in fact from a real mutual understanding was strikingly shown by an occurrence in Antioch, referred to briefly by Paul in Gal. 2 11—21. Paul and Barnabas had gone back to Antioch after the apostles' conference, and Peter too must have gone there soon afterwards. There, in the church composed of both Jewish and Gentile Christians, Peter seems to have taken part in the common meals of the church, in accordance with the Jerusalem agreement, suppressing his qualms about the ritual uncleanness of Gentile Christians. Now, however, there came Jewish Christians from Jerusalem, claiming the authority of James and reproaching Peter for having sat at table with the Gentile Christians, since, in the opinion of the extreme Jewish Christians, he had undoubtedly overstepped the barrier that the Law imposed on a Jew. Peter allowed himself to be impressed by these reproaches, and gave up taking part in the common meals; and his example caused Barnabas and the other Jewish Christians to do the same. Of course, that did not involve any interference with the Gentile Christians' freedom from the Law, but it did mean that the church at Antioch was split. Paul took Peter himself to task for his inconsistent attitude, and probably reproached Barnabas too (see p. 75); in any case, the result was that he left Antioch and went off without

Paul

Barnabas to pursue his missionary work in Asia Minor.

With that, it seemed that the incident was closed, and that no serious cause was given for fresh disputes, as Paul now went on with his missionary work in districts that were wholly Gentile; and so, in the account given in Acts, we hear nothing more for some considerable time of any differences between Paul and the Jewish Christians in Jerusalem. But the appearance was deceptive. In his letter to the Galatians, which was written five or six years later, when he had for some time been carrying on his missionary work from Ephesus (see p. 80) and had already been working twice in the interior of Asia Minor, Paul reacted to the news that since his second visit to Galatia, Judaisers had appeared there, claiming the authority of their connection with Jerusalem and the first apostles, and now, in the churches of Paul's mission far away from Palestine, demanding of the Gentile Christians that they should be circumcised and accept the whole Jewish Law retrospectively. Not long after that, we see that in Corinth too Paul's apostleship was being contested by the Judaisers, who asserted that he was not a genuine apostle, since he had not, like the first apostles, been one of the disciples of the earthly Jesus (2 Cor. 5 $^{12-17}$; 10-13). In his defence against this counter-mission, Paul did not attack the first apostles themselves; but he attacked the "false apostles" or "superlative apostles" (2 Cor. 11 $^{5,\ 13}$); and it is an obvious inference that the people responsible for this deliberate interference in Paul's mission were not the first apostles themselves, but probably the same extreme circles of the Jerusalem Judaisers that had previously, at the Council at Jerusalem, demanded that Gentile

132

Struggles

Christians should be subject to the Jewish Law. They had evidently not agreed to the peaceful settlement between Paul and the first apostles at the Council at Jerusalem, and were now carrying the struggle into his Gentile Church. That meant, of course, not only a breach of the Council's agreements, but also the endangering of the unity of the Church and a threat to the world-wide mission of Paul the apostle to the Gentiles. So from this point of view it was quite natural for him to act vigorously as soon as he heard of the counter-mission.

But Paul saw—and he was undoubtedly right—that beyond the Judaisers' demand that the Gentile Christians should become members of the Jewish religious community through circumcision, there lay a denial of God's work in Jesus Christ. That, indeed, had been the Jewish view which Paul had once shared, and which the Judaists were now propagating with fanatical zeal—that man is required by God to fulfil the commands of the Jewish Law, and that no one can obtain God's approval except by being as faithful and careful as possible in fulfilling those commands. Only the Jew who was faithful to the Law could thus stand before God, and so it seemed to the Judaisers a religious duty to make the Gentile Christians circumcised Jewish Christians, and so children of "our father Abraham". But that is exactly what Paul had recognised as the great mistake of his life—that he had thought, as a Jew, to obtain God's approval by his works within the framework of the Jewish religion; what God had now shown, by calling the despised and "godless" into the Church of Jesus the Messiah, was that what mattered to God was not the good works of the Jew, but man's readiness to trust himself to the seeking and saving love of God which had become manifest in

Paul

Jesus Christ: "So it depends not upon man's will or exertion, but upon God's mercy" (Rom. 9 [16]). What the Judaisers wanted was to win new members for the Jewish national religion; what Paul had recognised in the gospel as God's will was to free both Jews and Greeks from bondage to the world, and to make them free children of God (Gal. 3 [28]; 4 [3, 6]). So in the letter to the Galatians he contends, not against a different understanding of the gospel, nor against a false theology or false ethics, but against " a different gospel—not that there is another gospel" (Gal. 1 [6, 7]), and he contends against it with such passion that he goes so far as to say, "But even if we, or an angel from heaven should preach to you a gospel contrary to that which we preached to you, let him be accursed" (Gal. 1 [8]).

Indeed, in Paul's view, what the Judaisers wanted, and what they tried to do through their counter-mission in his churches, was not to destroy his life's work, but rather to annihilate the work of Christ himself in those Gentile Christians: "Now I, Paul, say to you, that if you receive circumcision, Christ will be of no advantage to you. You are severed from Christ, you who would be justified by the law; you have fallen away from grace" (Gal. 5 [2, 4]). That was no mistake on Paul's part: it was not a question of two different possibilities of Christian faith in opposition to each other, but of taking up once more, at another stage, the struggle between Jesus and the Pharisees. As the one who brought and proclaimed God's final act of divine salvation and his decisive and unconditional claim, Jesus had roused the hostility of the representatives of official Judaism, to whom the Jews' salvation seemed to be based on the fulfilment of the Law within the framework of the Jewish religious community;

Struggles

and now this Jewish national religion was asserting itself once more, with its reliance on the works of man, and against the gospel of God's saving work in Christ for all men and of his unique act of salvation as the basis of human action. Once more the pious man's illusion that he could merit his own salvation stood in opposition to the reality of the Church established through the resurrection of Christ and the sending of the Spirit—the Church of those who knew that "God is at work in you, both to will and to work for his good pleasure" (Phil. 2 [13]); and so what was really at stake in this struggle was not Paul's influence or success, but his Lord's cause. So Paul was not afraid to deal with the Judaising opponents in his churches in the most energetic way, so as to remain faithful to the commission that he had received in his call as apostle to the Gentiles. We do not know the details of the dispute, and in particular whether his letter to the Galatians put a stop to the influence of the Judaisers there or not; but the fact that it was kept and received into the later collection of his letters suggests that he was successful. It has often been assumed that Peter broke completely with Paul after their difference in Antioch, sided with the extreme Judaisers from Jerusalem, and took an active part in the counter-mission against him; but that is extremely unlikely; Paul himself mentions Peter later on in such a way that no kind of serious disagreement can be detected (1 Cor. 3 [22]; 9 [5]). Of course Paul's defence did not convince the Judaisers of the wrongness of their cause, and their hostility still threatened him during his last stay in Jerusalem (see p. 143).

At one place, Corinth, we can observe more closely the course of the Judaistic struggle against Paul even after the time of the letter to the Galatians, and here there

Paul

appears another opponent with which he had to contend. He had been working for more than eighteen months in Corinth, and then, after a short time in Palestine and in southern and central Asia Minor, he had settled down for a fairly long stay at Ephesus (see pp. 78, 96). There, probably some time after the Galatian crisis, he had news by word of mouth, and also a letter from the church at Corinth, which caused him to send that church a comprehensive letter (our 1 Corinthians) giving help and instruction in many detailed questions of faith and life. In that letter we can already see clearly that among those Christians, who came for the most part from Hellenistic paganism in its most varied forms, the old pagan thought was seriously endangering the Christian message. Christian baptism was regarded as the initiation into a mystery, and the baptisers were given much the same standing as the "fathers" of the mystery cults (1^{12-17}; 4^{15}); entrance into the Christian Church was believed to confer supernatural powers, and ethical conduct was therefore considered of small account (4^8; 6^{12-20}; 10^{6-13}); people saw the highest sign of divine emotion in ecstatic "speaking with tongues", and they even thought they possessed the resurrection and were thus free from the bonds of time (14^{1-6}; 15^{12}). Those Christians thus saw in membership of the Christian Church merely an easier way of acquiring supernatural powers and thereby fleeing from the world of fate and temporal things into the divine world of immortality where fear was unknown. So Paul had to keep on making it clear, from fresh angles, that the Christian is saved through the connection with God's historical act of salvation in the cross and resurrection of Christ, that he is saved, not by the possession of supernatural powers, but by the acceptance in faith

Struggles

of that divine act and by proving its truth in his life.

Apart from Paul's anxiety over the young church's continued imprisonment in the old pagan piety, the first letter to the Corinthians does not show that he had to face any real opposition in the church. Soon afterwards, however, the situation in Corinth must have changed fundamentally. Probably because of alarming news, Paul had to go from Ephesus to Corinth, where there was a sharp dispute with part of the church; and in that dispute he suffered a serious wrong from one of its members without being given any protection by the church (2 Cor. 2 $^{5-11}$). We cannot learn any more details about the occurrence, except that Paul went away in grief and then wrote a letter (which has been lost) "with many tears", which had the effect of making most of the Corinthians repent and decide to punish the guilty person (2 Cor. 2 $^{1-11}$; 7 $^{8,\ 9,\ 12-16}$). Titus, who had likewise been sent to Corinth, brought the good news to Paul, who had meanwhile left for Macedonia. Paul then tried, in 2 Cor. to restore the situation in Corinth completely, and as we read it we can see what the deeper causes of the dispute were. He still had to fight against the pagan misconception of the true character of Christianity (2 Cor. 7 ^{2}; 11 ^{5}; 12 ^{16}); but the opposition found its real strength against him in the arrival there of Christians who disputed his apostleship, reproached him with self-aggrandisement, and put forward on their own behalf the authority of the first apostles (2 Cor. 7 ^{1}; 11 ^{6}; 12 $^{16-18}$). We hear nothing of the demand that the Gentile Christians should comply with the Law, but it is quite clear that the Judaisers, by contesting Paul's apostleship, wanted to bring the Gentile Christians in Corinth too into direct dependence on the legalistic Jewish Christians in Jerusalem. It almost brought about a break between the church and Paul, and again it was only by emphasis on the revelation of Christ which had superseded God's old covenant, and on the Christian's consequent obligation of obedience to the heavenly Lord, that he was able to dispel the danger of a relapse into the old national religion of the fulfilment of the Law. Even at the time when 2 Corinthians was written, the danger had not been quite dispelled.

Although in Corinth the Judaistic opposition to Paul joined with the ties that still bound the Gentile Christians to the old religion of nature, it was only this Hellenistic danger against which he had to fight in the last letter that we have from his hand: the letter to the Colossians. The last missionary centre from which he continued to work for any considerable time had been Ephesus, and it is probable that his pupils had gone from there into the valley of the Lycus and had founded churches in Colossae, Laodicea, and Hierapolis. When he was imprisoned after his last return to Jerusalem (see pp. 143–145), he learnt of difficulties in those churches, and wrote from prison, probably in Caesarea, to the Christian churches which he did not know personally in Colossae and Laodicea, letters that were so much concerned with their common needs that he could wish them to be circulated among the churches (Col. 4 [16]). But the only one that has been preserved is the letter to the Colossians (together with the short private letter to the Colossian Philemon, which arose out of the same situation). Here we look into a church in which the Christian message had not really got the better of pagan ideas of worship. These Christians were still convinced that their lives

Struggles

were very strongly influenced by and dependent on a large number of potent spiritual beings of different kinds, without whose good pleasure man could find no access to the Godhead. So they clung to the veneration of angels, and believed that they could acquire a knowledge of the world of spirits through dreams and their speculative interpretation, so as to have in this way a share in the "fulness of deity". All this is clearly a variety of the *gnosis* that sought, through an approach to the spirits and through a speculative interpretation of the world, to safeguard itself against those elemental spirits. This form of *gnosis* was at the same time mixed with Jewish legalistic demands, involving not only the celebration of Jewish feast days and sabbaths and compliance with the laws about food, but also the practice of asceticism (Col. 2 $^{8-23}$).

It is obvious that there is here a typical mixing of religious ideas, and that these Christians did not think they could find adequate protection and certain deliverance in Jesus Christ. Paul describes this whole collection of ideas as human invention: "See to it that no one makes a prey of you by philosophy and empty deceit, according to human tradition, according to the elemental spirits of the universe, and not according to Christ." (Col. 2 ^{8}). Against such trustful devotion to supposedly potent spiritual beings and the fulfilling of legal commands, he emphasises that it all means a complete misunderstanding of Christ: "For in him whole fulness of deity dwells bodily, and you have come to fulness of life in him, who is the head of all rule and authority" (Col. 2 $^{9,\ 10}$). Christ is not only the revealer of the grace of God; as he has brought God's reconciliation, so he stands behind the Creator, and only in him can we have life and a share in God's kingdom (Col. 1 [13-15]). Paul therefore emphasises here, not only Christ's lordship over all the powers of this world, but also, with a greater clearness than we find elsewhere, his all-embracing importance in the whole universe. It is beyond doubt that, owing to the mixing of religious ideas by the false Colossian teachers, Paul gives to certain features of his picture of Christ a prominence that is not more than suggested elsewhere; but it is equally beyond doubt that, in doing so, although he makes use of all the mythical forms of expression of his time, he insists with particular definiteness that only faith in Christ whom God sent can give man contact with the saving reality of God, and that that faith implies, not the need of specially pious works, but certainly the believer's lifelong obedience to the heavenly Lord: "And you, who once were estranged and hostile in mind, doing evil deeds, he has now reconciled in his body of flesh by his death, in order to present you holy and blameless and irreproachable before him, provided that you continue in the faith, stable and steadfast, not shifting from the hope of the gospel which you heard. And whatever you do, in word or deed, do everything in the name of the Lord Jesus, giving thanks to God the Father through him" (Col. 1 [21-23]; 3 [17]). So in the struggle that had been forced on him by the Jewish Christians' hostility and by the Gentile Christians' lack of understanding, Paul upheld with complete consistency his Lord's cause, the commission that he had accepted on his conversion, and thereby kept the message of God's saving work in Christ from being perverted by emphasis on human works or by trust in human piety. But such faithfulness to his heavenly Lord settled his earthly fate.

9

THE END

AT the end of his last missionary journey in the east, Paul had reached Jerusalem (see p. 83). His further plan, as he told the Romans in the letter that was intended to announce his coming (15^{22}), had been to take to Jerusalem the gift of money sent by the Gentile Christian churches for the poor of the mother church there, in company with the delegates from those churches (see pp. 83, 95), and then to travel via Rome, where he hoped to stay for a short time (Rom. 1^{11-13}; 15^{24}), to fresh missionary work in Spain. It was not without apprehension that he went to Jerusalem: "I appeal to you, brethren, by our Lord Jesus Christ and by the love of the Spirit, to strive together with me in your prayers to God on my behalf, that I may be delivered from the unbelievers in Judaea, and that my service for Jerusalem may be acceptable to the saints; so that by God's will I may come to you with joy and be refreshed in your company" (Rom. 15^{30-32}). That means that Paul was afraid of two things in Jerusalem: the Jews might try to kill him, since in their opinion he had done serious harm to the churches of the dispersion; and the legalistic Jewish Christians might refuse to receive him in spite of the gift for the poor of their church, and in that case he might

Paul

even be frustrated in his intended missionary journey to the distant west. He did not disguise from himself that the journey to Jerusalem was going to be a fateful one for him. It is true that for this last part of his activity we have only the account given in Acts, and cannot check it by his own letters; and in the part of Acts extending from his arrival in Jerusalem to his departure from Palestine as a prisoner (21 ^{19}–26 ^{32}), the travel account that recorded the stages of his journey as far as Jerusalem stops completely till he leaves for Rome (27 ^{1}), so that for what happened to him during the latter part of his time in Palestine we have nothing but Luke's isolated narratives, very much filled out by speeches. About the end of Paul's life, Acts says nothing at all; consequently our knowledge of those last years remains extremely uncertain and fragmentary, and it is only about the decisive stages that we can feel quite sure.

First, Acts relates (21 $^{20-26}$) that James, who was now the recognised leader of the Christian Church in Jerusalem, but who evidently did not go all the way with the extreme Judaisers, drew Paul's attention to the fact that the legalistic Jewish Christians in Jerusalem had heard that he (Paul) had demanded of all Jews in the dispersion that they should give up following the Jewish Law. James therefore suggested to him that he should give a proof of his personal fidelity to the Law by bearing the legally prescribed costs of ending a vow that four Jewish Christians had taken; and Paul agreed to the suggestion, as he could show in that way—he himself probably having made such a vow a few years before (Acts 18 ^{18})—that it was not his intention to undermine their fidelity to the Law of the fathers.

There is therefore no reason to doubt that Paul

The End

actually did, on James' advice, make this attempt to dissipate the Judaisers' personal distrust of him (see p.38), and to do so was entirely in accordance with his principles, for he had never disputed the Jewish Christians' right to continue to live according to the Law, though he certainly had disputed the need to do so as a condition of salvation. But it is quite a different question whether the object that James and Paul had in view was actually attained through Paul's conciliatory gesture. Although Luke says nothing more about it directly, it is most unlikely that the extreme Jewish Christians, who could not be conciliated even by the delivery of the money collected, were persuaded to adopt a more friendly attitude by this proof of Paul's personal devotion to the Law of the fathers. In the further report of what happened to him in Jerusalem, we do not hear that the Christian church there exerted itself in any way to rescue the apostle of the Gentiles when he was in serious danger; for when he stayed in the precincts of the temple for seven days to fulfil his vow, he was seen by Jews from Asia Minor, who were hostile towards him because of the success of his mission in the dispersion, and was arrested on the pretext that he had profaned the temple by taking with him an uncircumcised Gentile, Trophimus of Ephesus, into the part to which only Jews were allowed access. That was obviously a slander, but a very dangerous one, for the entry of non-Jews into the forbidden part of the temple was punishable by death, as was recorded by inscriptions, one of which has since been found.

The false accusation, by which it was intended to get rid of the hated missionary, was followed by an uproar, which would have led to his being killed if the commander of the Roman cohort stationed in Jerusalem had not taken the alleged disturber of the peace into safe custody (Acts 21 [27-36]). But the Roman officer now saw himself faced by the difficult task of finding out the cause of the uproar, such causes often being unintelligible to a non-Jew. It is true, according to Acts, that he allowed Paul, before the case was heard, to address the crowd in Aramaic, and that Paul thus told his story, first of his conversion and then of what followed as far as his first visit to Jerusalem where he had confirmation once more, in a vision, of his commission as apostle to the Gentiles (Acts 21 [37]–22 [23]). It is, however, most unlikely that, in view of the excited crowd, the officer gave any such permission, the consequences of which could not be predicted; besides, the speech is clearly only a repetition of what had been told earlier, and the account given at the end about Paul's former experience in the temple may very likely have been passed on to Luke at second hand. It is probable that the officer, as Luke goes on to tell, had Paul taken to the barracks, so that the case could be heard in the usual way with the help of torture. But Paul appealed to his rights as a Roman citizen against being tortured, and the officer, who had himself bought those rights "for a large sum", at once forbade it. As it seemed to be a question of a religious dispute, the natural way of settling it was to refer it to the Sanhedrin, which was the Jews' highest court in temporal and spiritual matters. Luke's narrative of Paul's appearance before that authority, and of the dispute that took place there, seems to be a traditional account of no great value; and in any case the matter became no clearer to the officer. Now, however, things took a dramatic turn, which Luke describes graphically (Acts 23 [11-35]). A group of fanatical

The End

Jews had solemnly sworn to murder Paul at the first opportunity, and this plan was reported privately by the latter's nephew to the Roman commander in whose charge Paul was. Any accusation against a Roman citizen was necessarily in the competence of the provincial governor, and as Paul could be given more certain protection in Caesarea from Jewish ambuscades, the commander had the prisoner taken under military escort to Caesarea, the residence of the governor, and asked the latter to investigate and decide the rather difficult case.

So Paul left Jerusalem as a prisoner, and returned to Caesarea as a prisoner. There the office of provincial governor was held by Antonius Felix, a brother of Pallas, who was so influential under Claudius; he had as his wife the Jewish princess Drusilla, who was the daughter of the last Jewish ruler Agrippa I, and whom he had estranged from her first husband, King Azizus of Emesa in Syria; the Roman historians speak caustically of Felix's maladministration. Felix let Paul's case wait till his accusers had come from Jerusalem; these charged him with causing sedition among the Jews all over the world, and with profaning the temple—two exceptionally serious charges. According to Luke's account—which, however, can hardly rest on very detailed information (Acts 24 $^{1-26}$)—Paul emphasised in his reply that, although his views and theirs were at variance, he was an absolutely loyal Jew, and that the Jews of Asia Minor who accused him of sedition ought at least to produce their proofs.

Felix obviously saw that the matter was a purely Jewish dispute, and he therefore postponed his decision, leaving Paul under arrest but not in strict confinement; whether Felix and his wife really were at all interested

Paul

in Paul's message as Luke says, is very doubtful in view of their character. It is certain, however, that Paul now remained in Caesarea for two years (Acts 24 [27]) in an imprisonment that did not make communication with the churches impossible for him. So it is most likely that during that time he heard from the Colossian Epaphras about the difficulties in the church at Colossae, and that Onesimus, the slave of the Colossian Philemon, sought refuge in Caesarea with Paul, who, while he was a prisoner, converted him to the Christian faith. If this assumption is right, Paul wrote two letters at about the same time during his imprisonment in Caesarea—one to the Colossians and one to Philemon—which show that while he was a prisoner he took the keenest possible interest in the churches that had grown out of his own and his pupils' missionary work, and that he made every possible effort to bind their faith more firmly to Christ, and above all to teach them to base their daily life on that faith (see especially Col. 3 [5]–4 [1]). We see further from these letters that he had great hopes of being free once more and able to renew his missionary activity (Col. 4 [3]), that he intended, in fact, to go to Colossae after his release (Philem [22]). It may well be supposed that the disquieting news from Colossae induced him to postpone for a time his journey via Rome to Spain (he had intended to undertake it direct from Jerusalem), so as to visit first the Colossian church which was in danger, and which he had not yet visited in person, and help to base its life more firmly on the all-embracing reality of Christ.

But these plans came to nothing. When Paul had been imprisoned at Caesarea for two years, the provincial governor Felix was recalled owing to his maladministration, and was replaced by Porcius Festus (unfortunately

The End

we cannot be certain of the year of this change, and can only calculate that it was about A.D. 59). The case against Paul, which had been in abeyance during the whole time of his imprisonment in Caesarea, was now taken up again (Acts 25 $^{1-12}$). The Jewish authorities in Jerusalem made a formal request to Festus that he should hand Paul over to them to be judged in Jerusalem; but Festus replied by asking them to bring forward their charge in Caesarea, and this was done. As neither accusation nor defence brought any real clarification of the matter, Festus proposed that the proceedings should be transferred to Jerusalem. But Paul feared, probably rightly, that the danger to him from the Jews there would be too great, and so he made use of the right that he had as a Roman citizen, and asked to be judged before the imperial court in Rome. "Then Festus, when he had conferred with his council, answered, 'You have appealed to Caesar; to Caesar you shall go'" (Acts 25 ^{12}). That decision meant that, when the opportunity came, Paul had to be taken with other prisoners to Rome. How long he still had to wait before he could at last make this journey (though it was now to be as a prisoner) we do not know. It is certain that Festus had to send to Rome a report on the case together with the prisoner, and that he therefore had an interest in getting further information about it.

Luke now relates that just at that time Herod Agrippa II, who ruled over some northern territory as Rome's vassal, had come on a first visit with his sister Bernice (who was notorious for her immorality) to Festus at Caesarea, and that Festus took the opportunity to bring the prisoner Paul before the Jewish ruler, as the latter might help him to get a clearer picture of the real issues on which Paul was accused. After Paul had told of his conversion and protested his innocence in a long speech, their Highnesses, as well as Festus, were unable to discover any reason why he should be kept a prisoner, let alone sentenced to death. "And Agrippa said to Festus, 'This man could have been set free if he had not appealed to Caesar'" (Acts 25 [15]–26 [32]). This scene, which Luke constructs with special care, shows the Christian apostle proclaiming the gospel before the rulers of Jews and Romans, and is therefore particularly impressive; and it is quite probable that the Roman governor did call in the help of the Jewish vassal prince, to get a better understanding of the case, when he found himself obliged to form a judgment on the dispute. But Luke can hardly have had very accurate details of the interrogation, and Paul's speech is essentially only a repetition of what had been said before. At the same time, it cannot be doubted that, now that Paul had made his appeal to the imperial court in Rome, it would no longer have been possible for the governor to release him, even if for his part he had thought the prisoner innocent. "Acquittal is now impossible, after the jurisdiction of the provincial governor has been declined and the matter is in the hands of the emperor's court" (Theodor Mommsen).

Thus, when the opportunity came, Paul was taken with other prisoners under guard to Rome. Luke describes this sea journey in great detail, and as the narrative passes once more into the "we" form (27 [1]–28 [16]), there is no reason to doubt that he is again following the travel account and that his source is therefore reliable, even though he makes it more picturesque in places. The journey, on which Paul was accompanied by the Thessalonian Aristarchus as well as by the author of the "we"

The End

passages, took them past Cyprus to southern Asia Minor and Crete, and from there, although it was late in the year, further west. The ship was driven off her course in a severe storm, and broke up off Malta, where all those on board were able to find safety. They spent the winter there, and in the spring they went on past Sicily to Puteoli in the Gulf of Naples. Here, where the company set foot on Italian soil, there was already a Christian church, which gave Paul a friendly welcome. When he went on to Rome by the Via Appia, the Roman Christians sent delegates out to meet him as far as Forum Appii and Tres Tabernae (about 37 and 30 miles respectively from Rome), thereby showing him their delight at his coming. "And when we came into Rome, Paul was allowed to stay by himself, with the soldier that guarded him" (Acts 28 [16]). So, although he was in custody, he was not deprived of the possibility of working as a missionary in Rome.

With that, the "we" of Acts breaks off, and so does our definite knowledge of Paul's fate. Luke relates nothing more of Paul's contact with the Christian church in Rome, though he describes in a dramatic form one last collision with the Roman Jews (Acts 28 [17-28]), pointing out once more, as he closes, that salvation was by God's will turning to the Gentiles. Whether this account rests on one particular occurrence or not, Luke no doubt puts the scene at the end of his book so as to make it clear that the gospel had now finally reached the capital of the Roman empire and therefore the Gentiles; and he ends with the sentence, "And he lived there two whole years at his own expense, and welcomed all who came to him, preaching the kingdom of God and teaching about the Lord Jesus Christ quite openly and unhindered"

Paul

(Acts 28 ³⁰, ³¹). There can be no doubt that Luke assumes that after those two years Paul's situation completely changed; but he evidently did not want to relate any more, for he had carried out his intention of describing the course of the gospel from Jerusalem to Rome. The assumption occasionally made, that Acts was already written at the end of those two years, and accordingly Luke could not have anything further to write, is untenable, because the book could not have been written before the last quarter of the first century (see p.10)— a fact that follows from its connection with Luke's gospel, and from its undoubted distance in time from the events that it narrates. Moreover, Luke indicates clearly that he knows that Paul did not again go into the east after the time of his imprisonment in Rome, in fact that when the book was written he was no longer alive (see especially Acts 20 ¹⁸⁻³⁸ and p. 83).

We could therefore know nothing certain about the end of Paul's life, unless other sources than Acts told us something reliable about it. Now we have, in fact, in the so-called First Epistle of Clement, which is a letter from the Roman church at the end of the first century in the form of a rhetorically constructed narrative about the victims of wicked zeal, the following passage: "Let us keep before our eyes the valiant apostles: Peter, who, as a sacrifice to unrighteous zeal, bore not one or two but a great number of hardships, and thereafter as a confessor of the faith passed on to the place of glory befitting him. On account of wicked zeal and strife, Paul was crowned with the prize for the victory of endurance— he who seven times bore fetters, was a fugitive, was punished by stoning, and worked as a herald both in the east and in the west; he attained to glorious fame for his

The End

faith. When he had taught righteousness to the whole world, had reached as far as the confines of the west, and had given his witness before the rulers, he was thereafter released from the world and taken up into the holy place. He became the mightiest example of steadfastness" (1 Clement 5 [4-7]). As in conjunction with that there is mention of the victims of Nero's persecution, the impression has been given that the death of Peter and Paul is mentioned as having taken place before the persecution of the year 64. But it is extremely difficult to say how much Clement knew about the facts, for he speaks of the fate of the two "pillars" in such a way that they appear as fighters in the spiritual arena; and in doing so he continually uses familiar rhetorical turns of speech.

It thus seems, on a careful consideration of the details given about Paul, that the author of the letter used two pieces of information, which are not simply traditional, and which are therefore of some value to us: that Paul went as far as the "confines of the west", namely as far as Spain; and that he died after witnessing before the rulers. Clement therefore clearly supposes that his death was connected with a confession of faith before the authorities of the state, and it is only if that confession was made in Rome that it becomes clear why he should be chosen for mention in this connection. But did Clement know that Paul had in fact reached Spain? It is not for another hundred years that we hear of the matter again, in the oldest list that has been preserved of New Testament writings, a list which came from the church in Rome, and which is called the Muratorian Fragment after its discoverer Muratori. This list speaks of Luke's having left out of Acts any mention of Paul's journey from "the city" (meaning Rome) to Spain, because he was not present.

Paul

Of course, this is hardly independent evidence, as the person who wrote the list was familiar, not only with the letter to the Romans, in which Paul had spoken of his intended journey to Spain, but certainly also with the First Epistle of Clement, which had been written in Rome. So the only independent evidence that has come down to us is that of the First Epistle of Clement; and that evidence is uncertain, because we cannot tell, from the author's rhetorical language, whether he really had his own source of information about the Spanish journey, or whether he inferred it from Paul's letter to the Romans, with which he was no doubt familiar.

It is certainly not very likely that, some forty years after Paul's death, it was no longer known whether he had been released after his two years' imprisonment there and had reached Spain; and so we have good reason to suppose that after some activity in Spain he returned to Rome and died there as a martyr. In that case the conclusion that he stayed in Rome a second time as a prisoner, and that this second imprisonment ended in his martyrdom, is unavoidable, but there is nothing in the old tradition to make it certain. It is therefore equally justifiable to suppose that the journey to Spain was simply inferred by Clement from the letter to the Romans; and in that case we must conclude that the case against Paul, after the two years' Roman imprisonment reported in Acts, took a turn for the worse, and that he was condemned to death and executed. It is impossible to choose for certain between these possibilities; and so the only thing of which we can be reasonably sure is that Paul died as a martyr in Rome, at the beginning of the sixties, but probably not directly in connection with Nero's persecution of the Roman church. If so much

The End

that we should like to know about the end of Paul's life remains hidden from us, we must take the more care in looking beyond the person of the great apostle to his work.

10

THE WORK

PAUL regarded himself, first and foremost, as an "ambassador" whose task was to take the gospel of Jesus Christ wherever it was unknown ("not where Christ has already been named"—1 Cor. 1^{17}; Rom. 15$^{16, 20}$); and so he has taken his rightful place in history as the great missionary to the Gentiles. He was certainly not the first Christian missionary to the Gentiles, and he did not remain the only one, even in his own time; for even before him Hellenistic Jewish Christians in Syria had begun to preach to the Gentiles about Jesus Christ, and to receive them into the Christian churches that were growing up in the Jewish dispersion; and the Christian message penetrated quite early, independently of Paul, to Italy and Rome and probably to other parts of the Roman empire. But Paul was, as far as we know, the first missionary to realise fully that the preaching of Jesus Christ was a matter, not for the Jewish people or even for the Jewish religious community, but for the whole of mankind, and therefore expressly for the Gentiles too. He not only knew that he was sent as a dispersion Jew into the dispersion countries, he not only found, among his hearers in the synagogues of the dispersion, Gentiles already inclined towards Judaism, so that he almost necessarily

The Work

came into touch with people of Gentile origin; Paul realised from the beginning that God in Christ had not fulfilled the Jewish hopes of a king to reign over the Jewish people in the last days, but had "[reconciled] the world to himself" (2 Cor. 5 ^{19}), and that the gospel was "the power of God for salvation to every one who has faith, to the Jew first, and also to the Greek" (Rom. 1 ^{16}). That did not mean that either the Jews as the people through whom salvation was to come, or the task of winning them for Jesus Christ, had become unimportant; it was clear, however, that the task of the Christian missionary must now be, not to add new members to the Jewish people, but to strive that all may be "baptised into one body—Jews or Greeks, slaves or free" (1 Cor. 12 ^{13}). From this aspect, Christianity was revealed by its very nature as being no longer the religion of a people, however open it might be to the whole world, but the message which was meant equally for all peoples, and which must therefore be proclaimed throughout the inhabited world (*oecumene*, Rom. 10 ^{18}).

Paul, however, realising that the gospel was something entirely new in comparison with the old religions of race or nature, not only saw his task in terms of preaching as far as the "confines of the west"; he also regarded the individual churches which he helped to establish and to which he offered his help in building up their common life, never as groups of people entirely dependent on themselves, but always as members of the one body of Christ, as the "church of God" (1 Cor. 10 ^{32}). He made that unity a reality, not only through the connection of the churches with himself, being as the apostle of Jesus Christ the authority for all the churches (1 Cor. 7 ^{17})—

he gathered them into unity through the common bonds with the mother church in Jerusalem, the bearer of the tradition of Jesus (Rom. 15 ^{27}), by mutual help among "those who are of the household of faith" (Gal. 6 ^{10}), and by the interchange of leading members of the churches (Rom. 16 $^{1, 2}$; 2 Cor. 8 $^{22, 23}$). But above all, he reminded the Christians in the individual churches again and again that they served one Lord (1 Cor. 8 ^{6}), and that therefore in relation to each other they were members of one body (1 Cor. 12 ^{27}). By thus arousing and cultivating in the churches with which he was associated a consciousness of the unity of the Church of Jesus Christ, Paul became in truth the first herald of the world-wide Church of the risen Lord, the "Israel of God" (Gal. 6 ^{16}). And if Christianity, as it passed from the soil of Palestine to the world of the Gentiles, did not lose the consciousness of the unity of the one Church, it is largely the result of the work of Paul, who in this too might say of himself that God's grace toward him was not in vain (1 Cor. 15 ^{10}).

But Paul's work would not have been possible if he had not, like the acute theological thinker that he was, recognised the new nature of Christianity in all its depth, and so thought out the new message in all its essentials and guarded it from being misunderstood. For him, the former Pharisee, the relation between God and man had been characterised, as a matter of course, by God's demands in the Law and by man's fulfilment of them; and as a Jew he had taken it equally for granted that the same God had made his covenant of grace with the fathers and was for that very reason making those demands in dealing with the Jews. Now, however, Paul had been convinced by his conversion that God had made Jesus

The Work

Christ, whom the Jews had rejected and crucified, the heavenly Lord; that God had actually called the despised people into that Lord's Church, and so, by the act of salvation that he had carried out in the last days, had made that people his own. Paul was therefore certain that from now all knowledge about the relation between God and man must proceed from that divine act, that man was no longer to be asked first what he had done and was doing, but whether he allowed his life to be laid hold of and ordered by God's act of salvation.

That implied on the one hand that the Christian could not be tied down to compliance with the Jewish Law, and that Christianity was, by its principles, definitely separated from Judaism and established as a new religion of a different kind. It implied on the other hand that the Christian message was, strictly speaking, to be understood as glad tidings (evangel), that therefore at the heart of Christian preaching there was the news of God's historical act of salvation, which consisted in the cross and resurrection of Jesus (Rom. 4 [24, 25]), and that the fundamental question "depends not upon man's will or exertion, but upon God's mercy" (Rom. 9 [16]). Paul had actually experienced that life-giving new creation in the present; and, however longingly he was "straining forward to what lies ahead", looking for the appearance from heaven of Jesus the Saviour (Phil. 3 [13, 20]), he knew that the Christian was "transferred . . . to the kingdom of his beloved Son, in whom we have redemption, the forgiveness of sins" (Col. 1 [13, 14]). By clearly recognising that the Christian message was freed from any attachment to the Jewish national religion, and by concentrating the Church's message on the saving work of God in Christ which was to rule the present,

Paul

Paul took the Church of Jesus Christ, which he himself had so decisively helped to create, out of the realm of national religions, and put it on firm ground. As the Church of Jesus Christ was now a vigorous and self-reliant body, independent of Judaism, it could no longer be seriously shaken by the fall of the Jewish state in the year 70; and as Christians now knew salvation as sharers in the present work of God in Christ, the need gradually to postpone longer and longer the final coming of salvation could no longer seriously endanger the faith of the Christian world. So Paul not only had a decisive share in building up the Christian Church, but he also gave it the intellectual foundation that made possible its survival in the first serious crises.

In that way Paul's work was fundamental for the rise of the world-wide Church of Jesus Christ, and for its spiritual foundation. But that does not adequately describe his work. Paul had to contend with many opponents during his life, and quite soon his teaching was not only developed to serve this or that purpose, but also seriously misunderstood. But his letters, as far as they have been preserved, were the first writings of apostolic times; they came, together with the gospels, into the New Testament canon which was being formed in the second century, and through the centuries they have had more influence than any other part of the New Testament except the gospels. Time after time, when theological thought has taken a fresh turn, it has been rekindled by those letters (see pp. 1–5), and the attitude towards Paul's theology as shown in them divides religious denominations and schools of theological thought down to the present day. What is it that gives his letters, and through them his thought, such a far-reaching effect?

The Work

When Paul helped to create the Church, he did not base it on human organisation or any kind of human piety or good works, whether in divine service or in everyday life. On the contrary, he based it with unmistakable single-mindedness on God's salvation in Christ, bestowed by God on man once for all. But in the development of every church, just as in every Christian faith, there is a danger that man may take the central place, that creeds and liturgies, religious experiences and moral works may overlay or supplant the one vital thing, the meeting with God in the historical reality of Jesus Christ. But where Christians experience or have experienced this danger, they have met with Paul, and have been helped and guided away from it by him. So, throughout the history of the Church and of Christian thought, Paul has exercised a critical function as soon as the gospel was in danger of being smothered or forgotten. He was able to do this because he performed a fundamental work: when the young Church had come into existence through the experiences of Easter and Pentecost, he refashioned, in the way that the new experience showed to be necessary, Jesus' message of the early coming of the kingdom of God and the heavenly Son of man, and by doing so he preserved for the Church the message of Jesus in its essential features. By taking the Church and its theology again and again back to God's decisive act in Jesus Christ, and by trying to keep them from overvaluing human works, he kept them close to the Lord's own gospel. So it has been Paul's historic work across the centuries to turn men back to the Lord into whose service he had unreservedly committed himself. And today too, Paul still fulfils this task for everyone who is ready to listen to his message, whether we meet him with theological

Paul

questions, or simply with seeking hearts; "For I decided to know nothing among you except Jesus Christ and him crucified" (1 Cor. 2 ^{2}).

GENERAL INDEX

Abba, 92
Abraham, 118, 133
Achaia, 58, 79
Acta Pauli: *see* "Acts of Paul"
"Acts of Paul", 13, 14, 28
Acts of the Apostles, 5, 9–13, 29, 129, 130, 149, 150
Adam, 112, 113
Aegean Sea, 76
Alexandretta, Gulf of, 71
Alexandria, 32, 97
Amanus Mountains, 15
Am haaretz, 24, 51
Amorium, 75
Amphipolis, 9, 77
Ananias of Damascus, 48
Andronicus, 107
Angels: *see* Spiritual beings
Anselm, 116
Antakia: *see* Antioch
Antichrist, 109
Antioch in Pisidia, 73, 86
Antioch in Syria, 11, 12, 27, 53, 57, 70–72, 80, 94, 127, 129, 131, 135
Apocalyptic hope, 34
Apollonia, 9, 77
Apollos, 97
Apostles, 24, 54, 62, 125–132, 137
Apostles' conference, *see* Council at Jerusalem
Apostles' decree, 129

Apostleship, 54, 55, 67, 106, 126, 132, 137, 154, 155
Apotheosis: *see* Deification
Aquila, 78, 79, 82
Arabia, 49, 57, 70
Aramaic language, 72, 92, 144
Archelaus, 24
Areopagus, 11, 31, 74, 77
Aretas, 49, 50
Aristarchus, 148
Artemis, 82
Asia, Roman province of, 75, 80
Asia Minor, 12, 14, 20, 59, 75, 86, 127, 131, 132, 135, 143, 149
Assos, 83
Athens, 41, 74, 77
Atonement: *see* Redemption
Attalia, 73
Attis, 18
Augustine, 2, 55
Azizus, 145

Babylon, 20
Baptism, 48, 72, 81, 87, 93, 94, 105, 121–123, 136
Barnabas, 70–75, 129–131
Barth, Karl, 2
Baur, F. C., 4
Benjamin, 28, 30, 100
Berea, 77
Bernice, 147
Bishops, 87

161

Paul

Bithynia, 76
Blessedness, 64, 102, 109
Body of Christ (i.e., the Church, q.v.), 108, 121–123, 155

Caesar, 42
Caesarea, 80, 81, 83, 138, 145–147
Cenchreae, 79
Cephas: *see* Peter
Chamberlain, H. S., 3
Chosen people (*see also* Jews), 23, 34, 118–120
Christ: *see* Jesus Christ
"in Christ", 101–108, 139
Christianity, Hellenistic, 52, 53, 126, 127, 154
Christians, Gentile, 37, 85, 91, 125, 126–135
Christians, Jewish, 37, 82, 85, 95, 125–129, 142, 154
Christians, persecution of, 35, 46–52, 68, 150, 152
Christians, persons first called, 72, 107
Christ myth, 90
Chronology, 35, 58, 79
Church (*see also* Body of Christ), 1, 10, 27, 45, 55, 56, 90, 91, 120–132, 155–159
Cilicia, 15, 33, 59, 74, 80, 127, 129
Circumcision, 18, 22, 37, 61, 91, 128, 130, 132–134
Claudius, 78, 79, 82
Clement, First Epistle of, 13, 150–152
Collection for Jerusalem Christians, 59, 80, 83, 94, 95, 129, 130, 141, 143

Colossae, 138, 146
Colossian teachers, (false), 139
Colossians, letter to, 7, 8, 95, 138–140, 146
Converts: *see* Proselytes
Corinth, 14, 38, 41, 58, 68, 69, 74, 78–83, 86–88, 96, 132, 135–138
Corinthians, letters to, 9, 36, 38, 60, 81, 82, 88, 95–99, 132, 136, 137
Cornelius, 125
Cos, 83
Council at Jerusalem, 37, 57, 59, 74, 94, 128–133
Crete, 149
Crispus, 78
Cults: *see* Mystery cults
Cynics, 30
Cyprus, 29, 59, 71, 72, 127, 149

Damascus, 36, 47–50, 53–55, 57, 59, 69, 70, 89, 126
Danube, 17
Deacons, 87
Death, 97, 109, 110, 112, 113
Decapolis, 69
Deification, 108
Deliverance: *see* Redemption
Delphi, 79
Demeter, 18
Derbe, 73
Diana: *see* Artemis
Diaspora: *see* Dispersion
Dibelius, Martin, 7, 8, 24n, 58
Dionysus, 18
Disciples: *see* Apostles
Dispersion, 15, 16, 20–25, 27, 29, 35, 52, 71, 78, 126, 141, 154

General Index

Dostoievski, F. M., 42
Drusilla, 145
Dura-Europos, 20

Ecstasy, 71, 92, 97
Edessa, 72
Egypt, 20
Elders, 87
Epaphras, 146
Ephesians, letter to, 7, .8
Ephesus, 7, 13, 75, 79-83, 86, 135, 137, 138
Epictetus, 31
Eschatology, 35, 61, 62, 68, 85, 86, 109, 110, 113
Esdras, Book of, 23
Essenes, 25
Euphrates, 20
Exegesis, 32-35, 39, 61
Ezra, 21

Faith, 23, 55, 64, 65, 92, 94, 103, 104, 114-124, 138-140
Felix, 145, 146
Festus, 146-148
Flesh (contrasted with Spirit), 6, 40, 66, 112
Flesh of animals, 23, 91, 97, 98, 99, 129
Forum Appii, 149

Gadara, 69
Galatia, 74, 75, 80, 132
Galatians, letter to, 9, 57, 60, 69, 75, 81, 88, 95, 126, 129, 131, 135
Galilee, 16, 24n., 28
Gallio, 58, 78, 79
Gamaliel, 33, 36, 45
Gaul, 20

Gentiles, God-fearing, 21, 71, 78, 85, 91
Gentiles, mission to, 49, 50, 67-101, 119, 125-140, 144, 150-157
Germany, 17
Gischala, 16-28
Gnosis and Gnosticism, 19, 25, 35, 94, 103, 139, 140
God, Christian belief in, 51, 52, 60, 61
God, Jewish belief in, 15, 24, 34, 51, 60, 114, 115
Gods, heathen, 17-19
Gospel, 2, 29, 53, 56, 57, 60, 61, 68, 70, 88, 95, 97-99, 119, 126, 133, 134, 149, 154-160
Grace, 2, 3, 5, 23, 34, 56, 62, 91, 106, 134, 139, 155, 156
Greece, 12, 15, 17, 20, 74-82, 84, 86

Hagar, 32
Hannibal, 17
Hebrews, letter to, 6
Hegel, F. W., 4
Heiler, Friedrich, 104
Hellenism (*see also* Christianity, Hellenistic), 15-19, 71, 72
Hermes, 73
Hermes Trismegistus: *see* Thoth
Herod, 24n
Herod Agrippa I, 24n., 145
Herod Agrippa II, 147, 148
Herod Antipas, 24n
Hierapolis, 138
Hieronymus, *see* Jerome
Hippos, 69
Holy Ghost: *see* Spirit

Hope, 5, 34, 110
Hymn, 100

Iconium, 13, 73
Isis, 17

James, 57, 126, 128, 142, 143
James, letter of, 93
Jerome, 16, 28
Jerusalem, 1, 10, 15, 22, 23, 28, 33, 36, 38, 47, 48, 57, 59, 70, 71, 80, 83, 94, 95, 125–132, 135, 137, 138, 141–147
Jesus Christ, 5, 27, 29, 39, 41, 48, 49, 54–56, 61, 64–67, 88–90, 97–109, 116–118, 137, 139, 146, 154–160
Jesus Christ, death of, 56, 63, 89, 97, 98, 105, 116, 117, 121, 123, 160
Jesus Christ, expected return of, 61, 62, 68, 97, 109, 120, 123, 127, 157
Jesus Christ, resurrection of, 50, 54–56, 89, 103–107, 117, 121, 126, 135, 157
John, 128
John the Baptist, 26, 80
Josephus, 11, 24
Joshua, 30
Judaea, 24, 47, 49
Judaism and Jews, 20–29, 63, 73, 77–79, 113, 118–120, 125
Judaism, Hellenistic, 5, 15, 21, 30–32, 36, 71, 126
Judaisers, 125–138, 142–143
Judas of Damascus, 48
Junias, 107
Jupiter: *see* Zeus
Justification, 5, 114–118

Justus: *see* Titius

Kavalla: *see* Neapolis
Knowledge: *see Gnosis*
Koine, 16, 20
Kyrios: *see* Lord

Lagarde, Paul de, 2
Laodicea, 6, 138
Law, 1, 22–24, 27, 32–34, 36–39, 45, 50–53, 61, 63, 65, 66, 88, 91–93, 110, 111, 118, 119, 125–135, 137, 142, 143, 157
Lesbos, 83
Life, new, 64, 102, 105–109, 121, 122, 124, 157
Litigation, 96, 98, 99
Logos, 17
Lord, (*Kyrios*), 19, 53, 54, 65, 137, 139, 156, 159
Lord's Supper, 97, 122, 123
Love, 34, 92, 101, 116, 118
Luke, 10–12, 46, 59, 70–72, 74, 80, 83, 86, 144, 148–150
Luther, Martin, 2, 47, 51, 55, 99, 114
Lycaonia, 59, 72–75
Lycus, River, 138
Lydia, 76
Lystra, 73, 75, 86

Macedonia, 12, 15, 74, 76, 82
Malta, 149
Marcion, 1, 7, 60
Mark, John, 30, 72, 73, 75
Marriage, 27, 35, 36
Meat: *see* Flesh
Menander, 31
Mercury, *see* Hermes

General Index

Messiah, 34, 51–53, 56, 61, 63, 65, 72, 102, 109, 110, 120, 127
Metropolis, 80
Miletus, 83
Mission: *see* Gentiles
Mithras, 17
Mommsen, Theodor, 148
Monotheism, 40, 61, 85
Moral conduct, 15, 61, 93, 96
Moses, 34
Muratorian Fragment, 151
Mysia, 76
Mystery cults, 18, 19, 25, 93, 104–106, 136
Mysticism, 19, 25, 32, 35, 94, 97, 104, 105–109, 123
Myths, 19, 90, 104, 105
Mytilene, 83

Nabataean kingdom, 49, 69
Nacolia, 75–80
Naples, Gulf of, 149
Napoleon, 42
Neapolis, 76
Nehemiah, 21
Nero, 151, 152
Nietzsche, Friedrich, 3, 4, 51

Oecumene, 68, 155
Old Testament, 2, 3, 21–23, 32–34, 39, 60, 61, 85, 108, 111
Onesimus, 146
Orcistus, 75
Organisation, 87, 93, 94, 159
Original sin, 112
Orpheus, 18
Osiris, 17

Pagan thought, 136, 138, 139

Palatine Hill, 17
Pallas, 145
Pamphylia, 59, 72, 73
Paphos, 72
Pastoral letters, 6, 7
Patara, 83
Paul
   acts of healing by, 73, 81
   also named Saul, 29, 30
   arrest and imprisonment, 13, 77, 81, 106, 138, 143–152
   attempted veneration of, 73, 81
   character, 41
   contrasts in thought, 40, 62, 65, 66, 102
   conversion, 5, 10, 29, 41, 43, 46–66, 100, 112–116, 125, 140, 144, 148, 157
   death, 12, 13, 83, 150–153
   development of thought, 59, 60
   illness, 42, 43, 48, 63, 76, 105
   later influence, 1, 155–160
   letters, 6–9, 41, 81, 95, 99
   missionary work, 1, 9–12, 27, 49, 52, 53, 56–59, 66, 67–84, 127–142
   Nazirite vow, 79
   opposition to, 69, 73, 77, 79–83, 125–140
   origin and early influences, 15, 16, 21, 22, 28–40
   Roman citizenship, 15, 16, 29, 144, 147
   so-called "morbid concern over sin" 111–113
   sources of information, (*see* also "We" passages), 5–14
   style, 11, 30–32, 40, 41, 99–101

supposed marriage, 36
supposed second conversion, 50, 67
theology, 39, 40, 63, 64, 102–124, 156–160
trade, 37, 78, 88
Perga, 73
Pergamos, 75
Persecution: *see* Christians
Pessinus, 17, 75
Peter, 11, 17, 57, 59, 75, 89, 126, 128, 131, 135, 150, 151
Peter, first letter of, 93
Peter I of Russia, 42
Pharisees, 22–24, 27, 29, 33, 34–37, 51, 53, 66, 111, 113, 134, 156
Philemon, letter to, 9, 30, 138, 146
Philip the Evangelist, 83
Philippi, 76, 77, 81, 83, 87, 98
Philippians, letter to, 8, 81, 88, 98
Philo, 25, 32, 35
Philosophy, 17, 30–32, 40, 97, 99
Phinehas, 52
Phoenicians, 20
Phrygia, 73–75, 80
Pisidia, 59, 72, 73, 86
Predestination, 34, 60
Presbyters: *see* Elders
Priscilla, 78, 79, 82
Prophets, 24, 61, 63, 71
Proselytes, 21, 53, 71, 85, 91
Psalms, 24
Ptolemais, 83
Puteoli, 149

Rabbis, 23, 34, 35, 45, 47, 52

Reconciliation (*see also* Redemption), 68, 104, 117, 139, 155
Redemption and deliverance, 3, 18, 19, 89, 115, 116, 117
Resurrection (*see also* Jesus Christ), 56, 97, 103, 107, 136
Revelation, 19, 33, 39, 42, 50–56, 92, 93, 120
Rhea, 17
Rhodes, 83
Righteousness, 33, 46, 65, 90, 103, 110–118, 124
Roman empire, 15–17, 72, 154
Romans, letter to, 2, 9, 41, 60, 82, 88, 95, 99, 141, 152
Rome, 10–14, 17, 70, 74, 78, 81, 82, 93, 141, 142, 147–152
Rosenberg, Alfred, 4

Sacrament (*see also* Baptism and Lord's Supper), 25, 124
Sacrifice, 97, 116, 123
Sadducees, 24
Salamis, 72
Salvation, 2, 5, 34, 39, 53, 56, 63, 65, 68, 88, 89, 112–124, 133, 134, 136, 139, 140, 154–160
Salvation Army, 46
Samaria, 24
Samos, 83
Samothrace, 76
Sanhedrin, 22, 24, 47, 144
Sarah, 32
Saul: *see* Paul
Seleucia, 72
Seneca, 6, 79
Septuagint, 20, 21, 31
Sergius Paulus, 29, 30, 72

General Index

Sermon on the Mount, 61, 99
Sicily, 149
Silas, 30, 75, 87
Silvanus: *see* Silas
Sin, 2, 3, 39, 46, 64, 66, 111–113, 118, 119, 121, 123
Smyrna, 75
Sosthenes, 79
Spain, 20, 82, 141, 146, 151, 152
Spirit, 6, 12, 40, 44, 62, 64–66, 74–77, 92, 93, 100, 109, 113, 118, 121, 123, 135
Spiritual beings, supposed, 19, 39, 42, 111, 138, 139
Stephanas, 87
Stephen, 30, 36, 46, 56, 126
Stoics, 30
Suffering, 62, 103–106
Synagogue, 11, 20, 32, 46, 47, 71–73, 78, 85, 91, 154
Syncretism, 17, 139
Syria, 12, 16, 20, 59, 72, 73, 83, 84, 127–129

Talmud, 32, 35, 36, 40
Tanchuma, 34
Tarsus, 15, 29–33, 36, 48, 57, 70, 73, 127, 129
Taurus Mountains, 15, 73
Temple, 24, 67, 73, 125, 143
Tertullian, 14
Thecla, 13
Theodicy, 64, 66
Theophilus, 10
Thessalonians, letters to, 8, 60, 78, 96
Thessalonica, 77, 78
Thorn in the flesh: *see* Paul, illness
Thoth, 17
Three Taverns: *see* Tres Tabernae
Thucydides, 11
Timothy, 37, 38, 75, 87
Titius Justus, 78
Titus, 37, 82, 87, 129, 130, 137
Tongues, gift of, 92, 98, 136
Tradition, 4, 10, 47, 56, 57, 86, 89–91, 116, 126, 151
Transformation, 105, 108
Tres Tabernae, 149
Troas, 74, 76
Trophimus, 143
Tyrannus, 80
Tyre, 83

Universalism, 16
Universe, 139

Vegetarianism, 99
Verria: *see* Berea
Via Appia, 149
Virgin birth, 89

"We" passages in Acts, 9, 76, 77, 83, 148, 149
"We" used by Paul, 54, 87
Wesley, John, 2
Women in the Church, 38, 39
Works (contrasted with faith), 7, 56, 65, 115, 116, 133, 140, 157, 159

Xenophon, 11

Zeus, 73

INDEX OF BIBLE REFERENCES

Exodus		12^{25}	59	18^{10}	78
33^{19}	p. 34	13	11, 59	18^{11}	58
Leviticus		13^1	12, 71	18^{12}	58, 78
20^{26}	24	13^9	29, 30	18^{18}	79, 142
Numbers		13^{12}	30	18^{23}	80
6^5	79	$13^{16, 26}$	21	19^1	80
25^8	52	13^{21}	9	19^9	80, 86
Luke		13^{45-48}	86	20^{1-6}	12
18^{11}	113	14	12, 59	20^4	83
Acts		14^{8-18}	73	20^5-21^{18}	9
2	11	14^{19}	86	20^{7-12}	83
2^{46}	125	14^{23}	87	20^{13}	16, 43
3	11	$15-17$	58	20^{18-35}	84
4^{36}	71	15^1	128	20^{18-38}	150
5^{34}	45	15^{1-29}	129	$20^{22-25, 38}$	10
6	83	15^5	128	21^{11}	10
7^{58}	30, 46	15^{20}	129	$21^{19}-26^{32}$	142
8^1	46	15^{35-36}	75	21^{20-26}	142
9	5, 48	$15^{36}-16^{10}$	12	21^{21}	128
9^1	47	16^3	37	21^{23-26}	38
9^{4-6}	52	16^{6-10}	12	21^{27-36}	144
9^{11}	15	$16^{6,7,9}$	74, 75, 76	$21^{37}-22^{23}$	144
9^{19-30}	126	16^{10-17}	9	21^{39}	15
$9^{24, 25}$	49	16^{16-40}	76	22	11, 48
9^{27}	71	17	11	22^3	15, 33, 36
$9^{28, 29}$	57	17^1	9	22^{17-21}	67
9^{30}	70	17^{16}	41	22^{28}	16
10	11, 125	17^{22-31}	74	23^6	22
11^{20}	53, 71	17^{28}	31	23^{11-35}	144
11^{25}	70	17^{34}	78	23^{16}	33
11^{26}	72	18^3	37	24	11
11^{27}	71	$18^{6, 12, 13}$	86	24^{1-26}	145
11^{30}	59	$18^{9, 10}$	69	$24^{5, 14}$	91

169

Paul

24^{17}	83, 95	7^{13}	119	1 Corinthians	
24^{27}	146	7^{18-20}	112	1^{12}	97
25^{1-12}	147	8^4	93	1^{12-17}	136
$25^{15}-26^{32}$	148	8^9	92	$1^{14,16}$	68
26	11, 48	$8^{9,10}$	65	1^{17}	116
$26^{10,11}$	47, 48	8^{10}	108	$1^{21,23}$	154
27	14	$8^{11,17}$	107	$1^{23,24}$	88
27^1	142	8^{15}	65, 92	1^{24}	120
27^1-28^{16}	9, 12	$8^{18,26}$	62	$1^{27,28}$	51
	[148	8^{31-39}	100	2	34
28^{16}	149	8^{33}	104	2^2	160
28^{17-28}	149	$8^{38,39}$	64	3^2	31
28^{23-28}	86	9^3	28, 119	3^{11}	97
$28^{30,31}$	150	9^6	114	3^{22}	135
28^{16}	149	9^{14}	64	4^8	136
Romans		$9^{15,18}$	34	$4^{9,13}$	63
$1^{11,13}$	141	9^{16}	134, 157	4^{15}	136
1^{14}	68	10^4	119	5^{1-5}	97
1^{16}	120, 155	10^9	94, 157	5^3	44
$1^{16}-11^{36}$	95	10^{17}	117	5^9	96
1^{17}	2	10^{18}	155	6^{1-6}	97
$1^{19,20}$	31	11^1	28, 30	$6^{5,7}$	99
2^{14}	31	11^{11-32}	120	6^{12-20}	136
2^{18-20}	52	$11^{33,36}$	120	7	13, 36
3^5	64	$12^{4,5}$	122	7^{10}	56
3^{20}	34, 118	12^{13}	93	7^{17}	155
3^{21-28}	116	$14^{7,8}$	99	8–10	97, 129
3^{24}	115	15^{14-19}	41	8^6	156
3^{28}	118	$15^{15,16}$	68	8^{11}	98
4^{18}	118	15^{16-20}	154	9	98
4^{24-25}	157	15^{22}	141	9^1	54
5^3	62	15^{24}	141	9^5	135
5^{12}	112	15^{25-32}	95	9^{14}	56
5^{12-21}	111	15^{27}	156	9^{16}	68
5^{20}	118	15^{30-32}	141	9^{20}	88
6^4	93, 105, 107	16	82	9^{25-27}	31
6^{10}	121	$16^{1,2}$	156	10	123
7^5	66	16^7	107	10^{6-12}	123
7^{7-25}	111	16^{22}	9	10^{6-13}	136
7^{12}	118			$10^{16,17}$	123

Index of Bible References

10^{32}	155	4^6	60	1^{12}	56
11^{2-16}	38	4^7	63	1^{14}	33, 47
11^{17-33}	97	$5^{2,4}$	110	$1^{15,16}$	60
11^{23-25}	56	5^{12-17}	132	1^{15-17}	49
11^{26}	62	5^{14}	123	1^{16}	67
11^{29-31}	123	5^{16}	54, 62, 66	1^{17}	57
12^{12-27}	31	5^{17}	64, 107	$1^{17,18}$	126
12^{13}	121, 155	$5^{18,20}$	68	1^{18}	69, 126
12^{27}	156	5^{19}	104, 117 155	1^{19}	57
12^{31}	98	5^{21}	90	1^{21}	59, 70, 127
13^{12}	110	6^2	115	1^{22}	47
14^{1-6}	136	6^9	45	2^1	57
14^8	31	7^1	137	2^{1-10}	129
14^{25}	92	7^2	137	2^3	37
15	34	$7^{8,9}$	137	$2^{3,4}$	128
15^3	116	7^{8-12}	96	2^4	128
15^{3-5}	56, 89	7^{12-16}	137	2^9	128
15^8	50	8, 9	94	2^{10}	80
15^9	47	8^9	90	2^{11-21}	75, 131
$15^{9,10}$	44	$8^{22,23}$	156	$2^{15,16}$	115
15^{10}	156	$10-13$	132	2^{16}	34
15^{12}	136	$10^{1,10}$	41	2^{20}	108
15^{22}	113	11	70	3^{1-5}	44
15^{32}	81	11^5	132, 137	3^2	92, 118, 123
15^{33}	31	11^6	43, 137	3^5	64
15^{35-49}	97	11^{13}	132	3^{13}	90, 117
$15^{45,46}$	32	11^{18-22}	54	3^{21-24}	119
15^{51}	110	11^{26}	106	3^{22}	104
16^1	94	11^{32}	49	3^{26}	122
16^{21}	9	12^7	42	3^{27}	105
2 Corinthians		12^{7-9}	106	3^{28}	134
1^{5-11}	41	12^9	43	$4^{3,6}$	134
$1^{8,9}$	81	12^{10}	64	4^4	115
1^{13}	41	12^{16}	137	$4^{4,5}$	89
2^1	41	12^{16-18}	137	4^6	92
2^{1-4}	80	13^1	14	4^{13}	75
2^{1-11}	137	13^4	107	4^{13-15}	42
2^{3-11}	96	Galatians		4^{22-31}	32
2^{5-11}	137	1^{1-12}	126	$5^{2,4}$	134
3^{18}	105, 108	1^{6-8}	134	5^{2-12}	44

171

Paul

5^3	22, 33	3^{12}	109	4^{16}	6, 138
5^6	118	$3^{13,20}$	157	4^3	146
$5^{13}-6^{10}$	93	4^8	31	1 Thessalonians	
5^{22}	93	4^{11-13}	98	2^{15}	63
6^{10}	156	4^{12}	44	$2^{15,16}$	119
6^{16}	156	$4^{12,13}$	107	4^{1-12}	93
Philippians		4^{13}	64	4^{13-18}	97
1^1	87	Colossians		$4^{15,16}$	57
1^{18}	88	1	34	$4^{15,17}$	110
1^{23}	110	$1^{13,14}$	157	5^{10}	124
$2^{6,7}$	90	1^{13-15}	140	5^{12-22}	93
2^{13}	135	1^{21-23}	140	2 Thessalonians	
$2^{25,26}$	81	1^{24}	106	2	34
3^4	54, 66	2^{8-23}	139	2 Timothy	
3^{4-9}	100	$2^{9,10}$	139	4	84
3^5	16, 28	$2^{12,13}$	121	4^{13}	16
3^6	33, 47, 114	2^{19}	122	Philemon	
$3^{7,8}$	65	3^1-4^6	93	9	30
3^{7-11}	50	3^5-4^1	146	22	146
$3^{9,10,11}$	103	3^{15}	124		
3^{11}	107	3^{17}	140		